Dedication ✓ W9-CYH-586

It seems that every once in a great while, you meet a person who is like a lighthouse – a guiding light, always out on the edge for others, helping, protecting, aglow with enthusiasm. I have an old friend like that, whom I see only occasionally now, for he lives in New York and I live in Massachusetts, but I know his light is still burning brightly. Ironically, he spent most of his adult life guiding airplanes into New York City as an air traffic controller. I dedicate this book to him, my old boyhood friend, Howard "Buddy" Mansfield of Hicksville, New York, a consistent beacon of hope, joy and energy.

The Newport Tower, still standing in downtown Newport, Rhode Island, is considered by many historians and archaeologists to be America's first lighthouse. A fireplace on the second floor once provided light out two windows which shone out to sea and to the harbor mouth. It was possibly built by Scots explorers in 1380 A.D.
Painting by David Wagner, courtesy of Early Sites Research Center, Rowley, MA.

Copyright © Old Saltbox,1998   ISBN- 1-889193-02-X

Edited by David Garrett and Stacey Scanlon

Cover Photos: By Stephen Harwood.

Front cover photo of Nubble Light, York, Maine. Back cover photo of Pemaquid Light, Pemaquid Point, Maine.

Cover photos are available as note cards with envelopes, and as prints and posters, by writing: Steve Harwood, 30 Worthen Street, #B-11, Chelmsford, MA 01824.

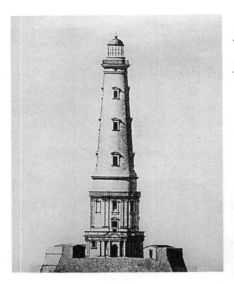

The Phare De Cordouan, off Bordeaux, France, built as a lighthouse, church and king's home in 1584 - the world's oldest sea-swept lighthouse.

The British Pharos at Dover, built by the Romans in the first century A.D., is still standing.

Ida Lewis, Newport's great lighthouse heroin, shown here in the rowboat from which she saved 28 lives.

Photos courtesy John Taft, Newport, R.I.

Introduction

As I write this book on lighthouse mysteries, I hear the distant moan of a foghorn blaring every few seconds from some six miles away behind my home in Salem, Massachusetts. The foghorn in Salem's outer harbor sits beside the lighthouse on Baker's Island and is heard only on stormy or foggy days or nights. I've been listening to it off and on for over sixty years, and the sound of it on dreary misty days is an integral part of the haunting atmosphere in this old Witch City. There were originally twin lights at Baker's Island, erected by the new federal government in January, 1798, and it was here during the War of 1812, that the lighthouse keeper saved America's most illustrious frigate, U.S.S. CONSTITUTION from destruction. Watching two British warships, TENEDOS and ENDYMION corner OLD IRONSIDES in the bay, Keeper Joe Perkins rowed out to her and informed the skipper that he would personally pilot her in amongst the treacherous reefs to the safe and fortified harbor of Marblehead. The British attempted to follow but a few cannon volleys from the fort and the enemy vessels withdrew. The incident was commemorated in 1998, when OLD IRONSIDES sailed once again into Marblehead Harbor to the applause of thousands of spectators, me included, and it was an awesome sight.

Baker's Island Lighthouse gained notoriety again only a few years after saving America's floating icon, when the great ship UNION wrecked on the island. The U.S. government had decided that Baker's didn't need two lights in the summer of 1816, so one was permanently extinguished. Returning home that winter with full cargo of pepper and tin from Pulo Penang, after almost a year at sea, the ship encountered a blizzard approaching Baker's Island. Navigator John Marshall explains the disaster in the ship's log this way: *"February 24, 1817 – thick snow from the North-East, hid the light. Light off lee bow, two cable lengths. To my great surprise, saw but one light. We thought we were at Boston Light, and the second officer said that we must go Southward of it. The second officer told the helmsmen he was wrong – headed West, and we struck. We were embarrassed by the alteration – there had been two lights on Baker's when we left for Pulo Penang out of Salem, but while we were away, the light on the Eastern end of the island was removed. The double lights were gone and a single light substituted. In the thick snow we grounded upon the sharp rocks. The main and mizzenmasts went over and the sea started breaking over her. At daylight she bilged, but the officers and crew got safely onto Baker's. Twenty distress guns were fired previous to leaving the ship. The ship's bottom was torn out, leaving a great quantity of pepper on the beach, and the block tin came out among the rocks where the ship first struck."* It was the first time in American history that a lighthouse had actually been responsible for sinking a ship.

Looking out to sea to the left from Baker's Island Light, one can see, on a clear day, Cape Ann and the mouth of Gloucester Harbor. Here, at Ten-Pound

Island, in the same year the UNION struck Baker's Island, one of the strangest encounters ever recorded occurred. First to spot the creature, *"resting, partly in and partly out of the water, on the eastern point of Ten Pound Island,"* was Lighthouse Keeper Amos Story. His sworn testimony reads: *"On the tenth day of August 1817, I saw a strange marine animal that I believe to be a serpent. I was setting on the shore and was about twenty rods from him when he was nearest to me. His head appeared shaped much like the head of a sea turtle and he carried his head from ten to twelve inches above the surface of the water. I should judge I saw fifty feet of him at least. His color was dark brown. I have often seen many whales at sea, but this animal was much swifter than any whale, and he moved in the water like a caterpillar."* After Amos Story, over 500 people reported seeing the sea monster, off Gloucester, Nahant, Winthrop, Lynn, Manchester-by-the-sea, Boston and Maine, from 1817 through 1820, also from the deck of the U.S.S. INDEPENDENCE anchored in Salem's outer harbor near Baker's Island Light. When the ship's commander, Captain William Malbone was told there was a sea-serpent off his port-bow, he laughed, thinking it was a joke, but he then watched the monster rise out of the water about twenty yards from the ship. Reverend Cheever Felch who was aboard, reported that, *"the serpent's color is dark brown with white under the throat. That there is an aquatic animal in the form of a snake, is not to be doubted. No man could now convince Captain Malbone that there is not such a being."*

Looking to sea to the right from Baker's Island Light, one can see Graves Light some twelve miles away, sitting like a lone sentry at the gateway to the islands of Boston Harbor. The 98-foot lighthouse was built in 1903 on ten acres of jagged rocks called *"The Graves."* They were so named because they look like a cluster of gray tombstones, and, in fact, have been the graves for many a mariner, who shipwrecked on the rocks. The channel beyond the lighthouse is called *"The Ghost Walk,"* because it is narrow and often enveloped in fog – a macabre entrance to one of America's busiest ports. It was here on the foggy afternoon of April 22, 1938, Keeper Llewellyn Rogers had an experience much like Amos Story's. He started seeing strange animals afloat by the lighthouse and some even climbed or slithered onto the rocks. There were monkeys screeching and jabbering, and serpents undulating through the water; cobras and large pythons, and soaked parrots and trumpet birds making a racket. The *"Zoo Ship,"* CITY OF SALISBURY had smashed into The Graves and was slowly sinking. Her passengers, humans and beasts, were diving into the water and heading for the lighthouse. She carried crates of tea, rugs, and bales of cotton and rubber-they too covered the ocean and started floating into Boston and Winthrop. Bostonians were drinking India tea for years thereafter, the rugs and rolls of rubber were sold by salvagers for high prices. Most of the animals that lived through the initial collision were captured and returned to the ship owners. Miraculously there were no human lives lost. The wreck eventually broke in half and the bow sank, but the stern remained on the rocks until the first nor'east storm, then it rolled under the sea to join the other half. It was considered the most spectacular shipping disaster in the history of Massachusetts, with a cargo worth over one million dollars lost. Whenever one visits Graves Light and listens to the hissing of wind and snow about the tower, one is reminded that the sound may not be from wind or snow, but from one of the escapees from the CITY OF SALISBURY that made its home in the lighthouse lantern room. Elliot Hadley, who was keeper at both Baker's Island and Graves Light in the early 1900's, said that Graves is a most fearful place and gets hit hardest in Southeast storms. *"I've stood on the bridge,"* he said, *"and looked up at the solid water rushing in toward the ledges. I don't know how far up the solid water comes, but I've been knocked down by it on the wharf beside the light, and opening a window to look out more than half-way up the tower, I've had as much as three buckets full dashed in my face."*

The lighthouse keeper lived a lonely, isolated life and as Keeper Hadley implies, it could sometimes become quite adventurous, if not frightening. Yet, I'm sure it was often monotonous, looking out day after day over endless miles of rolling sea, and at night, to constantly see only the light beam against the darkness. Some keepers, I'm sure, acquired a sense of solitude, whereas others wrestled with internal demons. It was of course the storms that kept the keepers on the edge of their seats, and all lighthouses were erected where the waters are most treacherous.

"It's not one gale, it's not two gales, it's not even twenty gales tied together by their tails that frightens you," explained one old keeper. *"It's what comes after, when the wind has had time to put a thousand miles of ocean into motion and turn it into a heavy ground sea. That's when you feel afraid. It rolls the boulders along with it that are down there on the sea bed; and when it strikes them against the base of your tower, the whole place quivers. You can hear them and feel them being thrown under the water against the foundation, rolling into it one after the other and making the tower shake; and you shake with it too, like all your teeth are going to be rattled out of your head. On and on it goes, and each one you feel you think it can't take one more thump like that. The next one for certain will be the one that'll bring the place down with a crash, and that'll be the end."*

A mile and a half further into Boston Harbor, in sight of Graves Light, is Boston Light on Little Brewster Island. It was erected in 1716 as America's first lighthouse. Canada's first lighthouse was at Fort Louisbourg at Cape Breton in 1731. The first lighthouse on the East Coast of North America however, may well have been shining on or before 1380 AD, but up to now there is no solid proof of this. There is, however, strong evidence that about this time, Scottish-Norse knights of the families Sinclair and Gunn, with the help of Venetian navigators, explored North America in and around New England, and actually settled for a time at Nova Scotia. It was once concluded that the Newport Tower, standing in downtown Newport, Rhode Island, was built by Vikings in about 1,000 AD, but now it is thought it may have been erected by Sinclair and his crew. The tower, which some believe is merely a stone built flour mill, used in the 1600s by Benedict Arnold's grandfather, has a fireplace on what once was a second floor and a window across the room looking out to the sea. This, many archaeologists and historians have decided, was an ancient lighthouse; the fire glowing out the open window to show others the way into Newport Harbor. All the experts on the subject are not agreed that this was America's first lighthouse but it might well have been. If it is, however, it would be most fitting, for one of the most courageous lighthouse keepers in America served a lifetime at Lime Rock Ledge, Newport in the mid-nineteenth century. She was considered a genuine American heroin.

Her name was Ida Lewis and she started her career at age twelve. Her father, Hosea Lewis was appointed Lime Rock keeper, but he was a sickly man, and only a year on the job he suffered a stroke. At age 14, Ida took over his chores as keeper, and all the locals considered her the best swimmer and boatsman in Newport. As a teenager she personally rescued thirteen people from drowning. When three farmers tried to save their panicked sheep that jumped off a downtown pier in a storm, Ida first saved the drowning farmers and then rowed out into the harbor, corralled the sheep and brought them back to shore safely. In her twenties, she saved men and women from sinking ships at great danger to herself, and at age thirty-one, she was made the official keeper of Lime Rock Light, replacing her father. She had already saved 23 people from drowning when in 1869, the President of the United States came to visit her at Newport. Stepping out of the boat at Lime Rock, President Grant got his feet wet. *"I have come to see Ida Lewis,"* he told the newspaper people accompanying him, *"and to see her, I'd get wet up to the armpits if necessary."* Ida was only 28 years old at the time, and she and the president spent many hours talking together sitting on the ledges at Lime Rock. When Ida was 64, sitting on those very same ledges, she heard a woman cry for help from a capsized sailboat. She immediately launched her rowboat and saved the woman from drowning-it was her final rescue. Said America's famous Admiral Dewey, who became a close friend of Ida's, *"I'm proud to have in our service a woman who isn't finicky about getting her hair wet."* On the day she died, October 24, 1911, after 57 years of lighthouse service, all the bells on the boats and ships at dock and anchored in Newport Harbor rang through the night. The skippers were tolling her memory as America's most remarkable lighthouse keeper.

The most remarkable lighthouse in American history is, of course, a lady too. Many don't realize that the Statue of Liberty in New York Harbor, facing out to sea at Bedlow Island, is a lighthouse. The flames of the torch were once tended by lighthouse keepers, and from 1886 to 1902 was maintained by the

American Lighthouse Board. Her lighted torch is reminiscent of the world's first and greatest Pharos Lighthouse of ancient Egypt, which stood at the entrance to Alexandria Harbor for well over one thousand years. Construction of Pharos began in 300 BC and was completed twenty years later. It was 400-feet tall with a statue at the top, and was *"admirably constructed of white marble,"* wrote Straboin in 24 BC *"It was built of several stories, for the safety of mariners,"* he wrote, *"to enable navigators coming in from the open sea to direct their course exactly to the entrance of the harbor."* Caesar, visiting Alexandria in 48 BC, said that, the tower at Pharos, *"was of great height and of wonderful construction."* Still being used as a lighthouse in 1154 AD, Arab geographer Edrisi, wrote: *"It is very useful, as it is illuminated by fire night and day to serve as a signal for navigators. During the night it appears as a star and during the day it is distinguished by the smoke."* It was said that the fires at the top of Pharos were visible at sea for thirty-four miles, but it tumbled in an earthquake in 1303 AD. Much of it remains underwater to this day. Archaeologists and engineers have discussed the possibility of raising it again as one of the Seven Ancient Wonders of the World.

Another of the Seven Wonders, strangely enough, was also a lighthouse, the Colossus at Rhodes. It too was built about 300 BC, and was the sculpture of a man, probably Apollo, holding a torch 100 feet high and made of bronze. His legs were spread apart and anchored by the ankles, and ships would sail into the harbor of Rhodes between his legs. This great masterpiece lasted only eighty years and was also destroyed in an earthquake. The bronze pieces, however, were salvaged and sold for scrap metal.

Another ancient marvel, the British Pharos, erected to a height of 80-feet on the White Cliffs of Dover in the first century AD, is still standing today. It and two other lighthouses were built to guide ships across the English Channel by the conquering Romans. The foundation of another of these three can still be seen at the far side of Dover village, and the third was the Tour d' OrDre at Boulogne, France, called by the British, "The Old Man of Bullen." It was part of a massive fort, restored by Charlemagne, and stood as a beacon faithfully until 1644 when it collapsed. In Medieval Britain, old chapels sitting on or above the sea doubled as lighthouses, displaying lanterns in windows that projected over the Atlantic. Some of these unique chapels survive, such as the one at Ilfracombe called Saint Nicholas.

Probably the most famous antique North Atlantic lighthouse is the Tour de Cordouan, originally built in the year 1200 on a 1000-yard long reef near the mouth of the Gironde River, Bordeaux, France. The treacherous reef is submerged at high tide and traders to Bordeaux threatened to stop coming for the wine if a lighthouse was not erected. It was at first a wood burning tower that was kept lit each night by a hermit, and then his assistant for over 100 years. In the mid 1300s it was rebuilt in stone, and in 1584, noted architect Louis de-

Foix, was hired by Henry III to build a grandiose structure that would be a religious, regal and residential lighthouse for the king. It took de Foix 27 years to build it, during which time, both he and the king died. When it was completed, however, it was a masterpiece, and never before or since has there been a lighthouse like it. The 100-foot tower stood within a great rock circular base, 135-feet in diameter, to keep out the raging sea. The tower itself, 70 feet in diameter, contained richly adorned and furnished apartments for the king, a chapel above, keepers quarters and fuel storage, topped off with the beacon, first a brazier for burning oak wood, then coal. The plush and decorative structure lasted almost 300 years, but was partially demolished by vandals during the French Revolution. It was then renovated and its lantern was raised to a height of 190-feet. The only other ancient lighthouse of Europe that could rival the Britain's Pharos at Dover and France's Tour de Cordouan, is Italy's Genoa Lighthouse, built about 1161. One of its claims to fame is that no other lighthouse in history has been struck by lightning as many times as it has. The Genoans were so upset by this that they had a local sculptor create a statue of Saint Christopher to stand beside the lighthouse but the lightning bolts continued to strike the tower and frighten off the keepers. One who wasn't frightened off was Anton Colombo, a brave and reliable man who served as keeper for years beginning in 1449. It was his nephew, Christopher, that, 43 years later, discovered America. The Genoa Lighthouse was badly damaged in 1544 by wars and was replaced by a 200-foot tower, which was finally provided a lightening-rod in 1778.

It is estimated that there were 34 lighthouses in the world in the beginning of the 17th century, mostly along Europe's North Atlantic Coast, and by 1820, there were some 250 lighthouses in the world, most along North America's Atlantic Coast. It was the American government's contention to have a lighthouse every twenty miles along the East Coast, making the United States the safest maritime nation in the world. Also in 1820, there was a new revolutionary invention by Frenchman Augustin Jean Fresnel. The Fresnel Lens for lighthouses was a remarkable cut glass design that intensified the beam of light from an oil-filled lantern, making it clearer and doubling the distance the light could be seen at sea. Within twenty years, all but a few lighthouses in the world had installed them. In the past, all lighthouses had burned wood or coal, or candles, but each had drawbacks. Lamps, wicks and whale oil was the choice of keepers in the nineteenth century, until the coming of electricity. It was this invention, however, that caused all lighthouse keepers to lose their jobs. By 1945, the Golden Age of lighthouses and their courageous, dutiful keepers was over. In that year, there were more than 30,000 lighthouses in the world. Within fifty years, most of these lighthouses have been closed down and boarded up, many of them rotting away where they stand, and those that shine the light each night, except for one or two, have been automated.

Chapter 1
Finders Keepers

The people who lived along the treacherous coasts of the Atlantic were not always the most pious and humanitarian folks that we might like to think they were. There were the Pilgrims, Quakers, Baptists and Puritans, but there were also the pirates, smugglers, wharf-wags, and wreckers. This later group resided, usually not far from the former, and in some ports, they mixed with the general population. Newport, Rhode Island, for example, was settled by Quakers, populated by the first Baptists, and frequented by the purest of elite society; yet pirates thrived there, smugglers flourished, and wreckers performed their evil deeds without resistance or retribution. Norman's Woe, Massachusetts, Nag's Head, North Carolina, The Isles of Shoals, New Hampshire, Cape Breton, Cape Cod and the rugged coast of Maine and Nova Scotia have their legends and tales of ships being lured onto the rocks by false lights displayed from shore by the fair citizens of the nearest town or village. The wrecking of passing vessels was often a community affair, the spoils that drifted ashore being shared by all that contributed to the deep deception. In many seaside villages a good wreck or two was needed to get them through a hard winter. For some, it was an age old and highly respected profession, handed down from generation to generation. Theirs was truly a "finders keepers, losers weepers," mentality. They saw nothing evil in luring a ship into dangerous waters with false lights. Usually the wreckers, also known as moon-cussers, didn't know any of the crew or passengers aboard the doomed ships for often the ships were from faraway foreign shores, containing strangers who didn't even know the local language. Fortunes could be made if a richly laden vessel could be lured in, and of course, wild seas and wind alone would smash a rich ship onto the rocks or force her into a nearby beach. Then it would be a free-for-all, smashing in the heads of any surviving victims of the wreck, to leave no witnesses of their greed, and carting off as much loot as possible to nearby homes. It is no wonder that when lighthouses were proposed up and down the Atlantic coasts, on both sides of the ocean, there was great resistance in many treacherous sectors, for the livelyhood of wreckers was in jeopardy. How could anyone suggest that lights be permanently erected to guide ships around rocky shoal waters, or into reef-strewn harbors? It just wasn't right-the wrecking of ships on the rocks was a natural phenomenon, an act of God, if you will, sometimes hastened by false lights, but otherwise, man should not interfere-or so thought the wreckers. The profession of wrecking didn't die easily, for they were not ready to disappear from the scene as quickly as the ships they had caused to sink under the waves.

It was about the time that the Pilgrims were landing at Plymouth, that England's Sir John Killegrew decided a lighthouse should be built on a hazardous cliff called The Lizard to overlook the Atlantic in Southwest England, but he met resistance from the local inhabitants right from the beginning. *"The inhabitants nearby think that they suffer by this erection,"* he wrote to a friend. *"They have been so long used to reap profits by the calamities of the ruin of shipping that they heavily complain on me."* But, even after Sir John managed to get the lighthouse built, *"with endless problems of recruiting labour,"* he could not keep his coal fire lit in the tower. *"I found it impossible to find assistance with the light's maintenance,"* wrote Sir John, and the wreckers finally had their way, for Killegrew's light was extinguished. It was replaced by a cow that roamed the nearby cliffs displaying a lantern on its back, to look like a sailing vessel, beckoning other ships to the rocks.

The most notorious haunt for smugglers and wreckers in England was the treacherous Scilly Isles, some fifty small islands and islets off Cornwall's Land's End. On Saint Agnes, one of the largest of the islands, an open fire was lit on its highest point on stormy nights for centuries. Until, in the early 1600s, a cresset container for burning coal was set into a lantern and erected on a long pole, which remained constantly lit for some eight decades. A sixty-foot tower lighthouse was built in 1680, and on top of the tower was a glazed lantern, standing 200 feet above the sea. Of the 1,000 plus inhabitants of the Scillys, a good fifty percent were opposed to the lighthouse, and if its keeper should leave the coal fire at any time, it seems that it would inevitably be snuffed out by some unseen hand carrying a bucket of water. Such was the case on the evening of October 22, 1707, when four richly laden ships were spotted from shore, returning in glory with the treasures of Toulon. It was the third day of stormy weather and the skippers were not sure of their position. There was no light to guide them, and when the Gilstone Ledges loomed, it was too late to escape. The EAGLE, ROMNEY, FIREBRAND and the 96-gun flagship ASSOCIATION all smashed into the rocks and sank. The only survivor of the flagship was the admiral of the fleet, Sir Cloudesley Shovell, who managed to swim from Bishop's Rock where his vessel sank, to the island shore. As he crawled up the beach, shouting for help, a tough woman wrecker clouted him over the head with his namesake and then stripped him of his jeweled rings. Over 2,000 officers and crewmen from the four ships were killed, most drowned, but some murdered by the wreckers like their admiral. Much treasure washed ashore and was collected by the islanders, but more was confiscated from the sunken wrecks when scuba divers found two of them underwater, including the ASSOCIATION in 1968. Over 800 gold coins, 4,000 silver coins, bronze cannons, gold rings, silver spurs, dagger hilts, silver eating utensils, along with a silver toothpick case and a silver plate displaying the Shovell coat-of-arms, have been thus far salvaged, under the guiding light of the Bishop Rock Lighthouse built over the flagship wreck in 1851. It is said on the Scilly Isles that Admiral Shovell made many an islander a millionaire. Another oft quoted saying on the island is, *"Save a stranger from the sea and you have found a new enemy."* Thus, the wreckers of the Scillys hardly ever reported to the mainland authorities of finding survivors from the many ships that smashed into their granite rocks. It has also been suggested in Britain that along the north coast of Cornwall, even the clergy once took an active part in benefiting from illicit shipwreck salvage.

According to old William Blindloss, the man who built South East Lighthouse on Block Island, Rhode Island, on this side of the Atlantic, the clergy also took an interest in wrecking. Blindloss said that in the late 1600s, when rumor on the mainland was that the islanders had taken to wrecking to make ends meet, preacher Seth Baldwin was sent over to keep the Block Islanders on the straight and narrow path. The islanders listened to his preaching, *"but it didn't change them none,"* and *"they never put a penny into the preacher's hat when his sermon was done."* *"Soon"*, reported Blindloss, *"the preacher was but skin and bones, near starving to death from lack of funds to buy food."* Preacher Baldwin finally complained and a town meeting was set to discuss what to do. *"Could each family give the preacher a potato or a squash, or a turnip or two–the answer was no."* They could not spare any food. *"They could,"* they concluded, *"only give the preacher a special hook."* Every islander had a pole with a bent nail on the end of it, called hooks, that were used to fish items out of the water from shipwrecks. It had long ago been agreed that everyone's hook had to be the same length, so that no one would have an added advantage of hooking shipwreck flotsam from the shore. Out of the goodness of their hearts the Block Islanders finally decided that *"Preacher Baldwin could have a hook-pole one inch longer than theirs, and if he couldn't support himself with that, he could starve to death."*

One of the great characters of Block Island history was Old Chrissy, a Dutch woman who was shipwrecked on Block Island in the early 18th century, and built a shack right where she landed after being rescued by wreckers. She lived there for many long years, making a living off the sea by fishing and wrecking. It is said that she would wade out waist deep into the surf to collect cargo and treasures from ships she had lured into the rocks with false lights. She'd lift her skirt with one hand, to keep it dry, and carry a club in the other, which she'd use to silence any survivors she might encounter floating on the surface waters. She was so successful in coaxing ships in to their doom, and so ruthless in her manor, that she inspired a gang of cutthroat followers, known as "Chrissy's Gang." One day, however, her teammates thought she went too far. While searching through the flotsam of a shallow water wreck, Old Chrissy came upon a half drowned man floating face up and crying for help. Chrissy recognized him as her oldest son Edward, who had left Block Island without her permission and had gone to sea as a merchant sailor. *"It's me, Ma,"* said Edward, seeing his mother standing over him. *"I know,"* she said, and she came down with the club, whacking her son in the head and killing him. When asked to explain her cruel action by her followers, Chrissy replied, *"A son is but a son, but a wreck is survival."*

In many seaside communities, wrecking gangs competed with each other and fought over shipwrecks. In places like Aldeburgh, Suffolk, England, two wrecker gangs built rival lookout towers on either end on the beach, to hopefully be the first to spot and plunder a wreck before the rival gang could get to it. In some communities this fierce competition for wreck salvage lasted well into the twentieth century. In most cases wrecking gangs cared little for saving human lives, and in some cases, like Old Chrissy's gang, they preferred snuffing out the last breath of any survivors, following the old pirates' philosophy of, *"Dead men tells no tales."*

The avarice of wreckers came to light only a few miles from the Nova Scotia capital of Halifax in 1853, when the luxury steamer HUMBOLT wrecked at Portuguese Cove. Local citizens attacked the wrecked steamer like a swarm of locusts and carried off every moveable object aboard the vessel, but didn't lift a hand to help survivors. The authorities were helpless and later tried to pass a law making wrecking a crime, but without success. It was six years later, however, when the selfish greed of wreckers was brought to public attention again in Nova Scotia and resulted in new strong legislation. The steamer INDIAN was sailing from England to Portland, Maine on November 21, 1859 and struck Seal Ledges, halfway between Cape Breton and Halifax. After an hour of being buffeted by the surf, the INDIAN split in two, her bow and aft sections falling over, wedged firmly in the ledges. She was near the village of Marie Joseph, and even with the cold and brisk wind, men in small boats came out from the village to circle the wreck. Aboard the wreck, passengers and crew were pleading for help, but the wreckers in their small boats were not there for rescue, but for plunder. All the small boats were within hailing distance, but they did not attempt to help the survivors. The wreckers were waiting until all aboard died of exposure or drowned. Life-saving dories did finally come hours later and rescued some people, but the wrecker gangs in their little boats merely rowed and sailed about like birds of prey, until the rescue was completed, waiting until all had left the ship or died. Then, they swooped in, fighting among themselves for the treasures left behind. They looted all personal luggage and the captain's locker, stripping the steamer to the bone. The Canadian people were infuriated when they heard of it, and new laws were soon on the books making wrecking a crime with stiff penalties. It was the gallows for those who in any way harmed a survivor of a shipwreck, or placed a survivor in jeopardy while salvaging from a vessel.

It was, however, established on or about the same time, in the House of Assembly of Nova Scotia, the establishment of laws pertaining to wrecks and wreckers on a 28 mile long and 2 mile wide spit of land called Sable Island. It read as follows: *"The superintendent of the island, as a stimulus to ascertain in case of wrecks, a percentage on property saved has always been allowed, and also a small sum to each of the men employed at any wreck. It shall be considered a part of the ordinary duty, for which both superintendent and men are paid and supported, and for which no extra claim should be made. The bounty, in case of wrecks, is given as a stimulus in effort to save life and property."*

So, in mid-nineteenth century Canada, wreckers were being slapped with one official hand, and encouraged to plunder with another. Unfortunately for the victims of wrecks at Sable Island, Nova Scotia, the wreckers who camped on the pickle-shaped strip for the sole purpose of receiving shipwreck bounty, had little fodder for themselves, and weren't inclined to save and suckle survivors. It was, however, necessary for survival of people and property from wrecks that the government paid wreckers a percentage of all cargo they were able to salvage, for resale in Halifax. With an official superintendent on the island, he would maintain order among the wrecking gangs and help to get cargo ashore before it went under or spoiled. Then it was transported to the mainland, which wasn't an easy chore, for the weather at Sable was often wild, and the surrounding shoal waters contain a sandy substance like quicksand that quickly swallows stranded vessels and their contents. Sea-soaked perishables such as flour, salt, or other foodstuffs, weren't worth the wreckers while, and if some foodstuffs were brought ashore to the island dry, and the mainland transport vessels weren't available, or couldn't get into Sable because of foul weather, the food would spoil and all the wreckers' toil would be in vain. The wreckers of Sable Island, constantly numbering between 30 to 40 men, were described by one Island Superintendent as *"desperate, violent men, who would stop at nothing to line their pockets, including murder."*

Prior to the twentieth century, the Humane Society had established a foothold at Sable Island and sturdy lifeboats were provided for the superintendent and his assistants to save shipwreck victims and vessel valuables. All wrecking carried out at the treeless sandy island today is government sponsored and continues to be quite profitable. Although the Canadian government allows no outsiders on the island today, but for those who attend the two lighthouses that adorn either end, and the lifesaving station, a total of about twenty people. It is ironic that Sable was the first North American land ever populated by Europeans. In 1598, 48 French convicts were dropped off there and left to fend for themselves. Within five years, all had been murdered but eleven, who made a truce and began to live peaceful, eating seals and looting shipwrecks. The French government eventually returned the eleven back to France, but they pleaded with the king to be allowed to live out their lives on Sable Island, to which he agreed. The convicts then made a fortune from wrecks and from exporting *"sea-horse teeth"* to Europe, which are better known today as walrus tusks.

As wild and windy as Sable Island is, man and beast, it seems, miraculously survived there over the centuries. Some 300 wild ponies roam the sand dunes today, thought to be either cargo of an eighteenth century shipwreck, or possibly descendants of horses purposely deposited there in 1760 by the wealthy Boston merchant, Thomas Hancock, uncle of patriot John Hancock, "to aide shipwreck victims." Hancock never specified if the survivors were supposed to ride the horses or eat them. Wild cows once grazed the island, left there by the Portuguese in the 1500s, as did wild pigs, remnants of a shipwreck, who were noted for eating bodies that washed ashore from shipwrecks in the late 1700s. Rats from stranded ships infested the island from 1884 through 1896, when the only solution to rid the island of them, it seemed, was to import domestic cats from Halifax. The cats solved the rat problem within a year or two, but the glut of cats managed to kill off the island rabbit population as well, and even today, a few wild cats of evil nature, roam the island. How all these animals survive on this giant sandbank is a true mystery, but it is obvious that man always survived on this island by the treasures brought forth by shipwrecks, and is why no visitors are allowed on the island by the government to this day. Although the life of a wrecker is often a grueling, unrewarding one, occasionally a Sable Islander strikes it rich, gathering in the items spewed up from the raging surf which is littered with some 560 shipwrecks.

Superintendent Philip Dodd uncovered a large stash of silver and gold from a sand dune in 1884, possibly buried there by pirates, but more than likely cargo from an old shipwreck that had been covered by sand. The find was kept secret at the time, Dodd reporting it only to his superiors. The government sent soldiers to the island to recover it, presenting Dodd with a stipend for finding it. It was said to be worth a *"King's ransom,"* but for Dodd it wasn't a case of finders keepers, and the British government never rightly showed their appreciation. Earlier in this century, an assistant lighthouse keeper found a large bundle of English bank notes protruding from a sandbank. They were all 200 pound notes, worth a small fortune. The assistant keeper left the island on the next boat for Halifax and started a clothing business there, which is thriving to this day.

As the surf and currents continue to move the island sands at a steady pace southeast at one-eighth of a mile per year, old forgotten or never discovered wrecks appear out of the dunes, some revealing fortunes in gold, silver, gems and artifacts. The Canadian government representatives are forever watchful at Sable Island, especially after a heavy storm, never knowing what new delights the shifting sands and thundering surf might reveal. Since 1919, the western end of Sable Island has lost an estimated 14 miles, which has been naturally added to the east-end. The 70-feet high West End Lighthouse built in 1872, has been forced to move and has been rebuilt five times as the East Light is steadily being forced into the center of the island from the movement of sand. Says one of the last keepers of the East Light, Frank Tanner, *"Items are being constantly exposed in the sand, and it's always fascinating to hike along the beach, for you never know what you'll find. There must be two million in treasure sunken around here."*

It is interesting to note that when lighthouses were erected at either end of the Sable sand crescent in the mid-1870s, their presence in no way reduced the number of shipwreck disasters off the island. As island historian, Allison Mitcham points out, *"In the decade before the building of the lighthouses and the decade afterwards, there had been nearly the same number of wrecks. The lights, it would seem, had neither lured unsuspecting mariners onto the island, as early detractors had feared; nor had they, apparently, been seen in time by captains disoriented in fog, or snow or driving rain."*

Keeper Frank Turner, who has now been replaced at the East Light by automation, tells us, since the first murderous convict settlers, *"Sable has always had a grisly reputation."* His favorite island story, told on cold stormy nights at the lighthouse, is that of the *"weeping woman phantom."* It is a true story of theft and gore concerning wreckers, that has become part of the legend and lore of the island. In the Sable Island story, the victim is Mrs. Elizabeth Copeland, the beautiful wife of Doctor James Copeland, surgeon of the British Seventh Regiment of Foot, stationed at Halifax in the late 1700s. The Copelands were two of 200 passengers aboard the ship PRINCESS AMELIA, bound for Prince Edward Island for settlement, at the bequest of Prince Edward himself. Besides the prospective settlers, the military escort and their families, there was a small fortune in silver aboard to finance the new settlement. A severe storm forced the ship off course and she smashed into Sable, sinking within a few minutes and drowning all but a few, including Mrs. Copeland who floated ashore on a hatch-cover. Wreckers were waiting for them and for all treasures that washed ashore in the breakers. Survivors were immediately clubbed when they hit the beach and their pockets and clothes searched for valuables. Mrs. Copeland was allowed to live only because she was beautiful and the wrecker leader took a liking to her. He dragged her back to his hut. It was then that he noticed the emerald ring she wore on her left hand, but because her finger was swollen, he couldn't remove it. Before she completely recovered consciousness from her shipwreck ordeal, the wrecker sliced off her finger and pocketed the ring with her finger still attached to it. Blood squirted form her finger stump and she moaned in agony, the screeching from her, driving the wrecker from his own hut. With the precious ring to sell on the mainland, he was not anxious to stay on Sable, and he sailed away once the storm subsided. The shipwrecked woman he left behind would die of starvation he supposed, or possibly still be alive to do his pleasure when he returned. She did survive, but went insane from the torment and torture she had endured. Weeks later, Captain Edmund Torrens, with a substantial crew was sent out from

Halifax on the schooner HARRIOT to find the missing PRINCESS AMELIA and her passengers. However, Sable Island also swallowed up the HARRIOT in a second storm, and again, only one person survived the shipwreck, and that was Edmund Torrens. Two hours after the schooner went down, Torrens' dog managed to swim ashore, half dead. Torrens revived him, then built a hut for them to escape the elements. The HARRIOT had wrecked on the west end of the island and when the weather cleared, Torrens and his dog trekked to the east side, where he found wreckage from the PRINCESS AMELIA. With dusk coming on and another storm in the wind, Captain Torres didn't have time to make it back to his hut at the west end, so he walked inland and found a wreck-er's hut with a fireplace and stacked firewood. His dog would not enter the hut and growled at something moving inside. Torrens, exhausted and cold, entered the hut and started a fire with flint found on a table inside. In the light from the flames the Captain then noticed a figure in the corner of the room, not cower-ing or hiding, but boldly staring at him with fierce green eyes. She combed her long snarled strawberry hair with a stick. Torrens was startled and asked who she was, but she answered only by moaning. The dog outside the door contin-ued to growl. The woman then pointed to her bloody stub of a finger and she began weeping until a chill crept up the Captain's back. He dare not move too close to her, for she looked wild and demented, but he continued to question her as he threw more wood on the fire to see her more clearly. She continued to weep, yet her eyes were raging. When Torres left the hut to coax his dog in to dry by the fire, the dog continued to back off and whimper. When he finally caught the dog and brought it into the hut, the woman had disappeared, run off, Torrens suspected, but later, questioned himself as to whether the woman was real or not. He thought she might have been a ghost or a phantom. When he was rescued and returned to Halifax, he made his official report on the PRINCESS AMELIA'S destruction. It was then that he realized the woman, whether she was a ghost or real, was Doctor Copeland's wife. Friends of hers in Halifax told Torrens of her beautiful emerald ring, and the Captain then real-ized that it had been torn from her finger and that was what the suffering woman had been trying to tell him. If it was stolen by wreckers, which Torrens surmised, he knew where to look for it. Months later, visiting a pawn-broker shop at Cape Breton, he found the emerald ring, pawned for just twenty shillings by a wrecker. Torrens was then able to track down the wrecker at a local pub and have him arrested for murder. Although the culprit's name has been lost to time, Captain Torrens saw to it that justice was done and the wrecker was eventually hanged for his crime. Yet, no one knows if Mrs. Copeland was murdered, or was left to roam the dunes a demented banshee who would cry and howl throughout the nights for those few who live on the island to hear. Without fail on moonlit nights, some would occasionally see her cowering near one of the old wrecker shacks or by the ribs of some old ship relic. According to Keeper Tanner, *"You can hear the rustling of her dress as she hurries from one place to another in the old, deserted West End Lighthouse, which is her favorite haunt, and if you listen closely, you can hear her weeping, I've never seen her."* He reports, *"but once I did see those angry green eyes squinting down at me from the top of those winding lighthouse stairs."* By the way, Tanner concluded, *"The great fortune in the PRINCESS AMELIA has never been found."*

Some 135 miles straight north from Sable, is Scatarie Island, which is seven miles long, three miles wide and only six miles off the Cape Breton coast. It is also considered an old wrecker's paradise and place of plunder. It was the first landfall for immigrants who came to North America from the British Isles by the droves in the early eighteen hundreds. Some hit the island head on, their vessels striking beneath their feet. A few managed to swim ashore, only to be met with desolation and exposure to the elements, especially in the winter. Wreckers here took on the guise of seal hunters, visiting the island in the early spring, looking to slaughter seals, but also to slaughter shipwreck victims, if any still were alive after being stranded on the island for months without shelter or provisions. Usually it was easy pickings for the seal-hunter-wreckers to just sort through items washed ashore from the wrecks, and through the pockets and purses of frozen victims. Many times because of icebergs or rough water, shipwreck survivors couldn't make it across the waters to the village of Main-a-Dieu, only a few miles away on the mainland and died of exposure or starved only to be picked over by vulturous seal hunters in the early spring. This was all before villagers even realized that there had been a shipwreck on the island. As early as 1829, the noted Canadian Judge, Thomas Haliburton, pleaded with the Canadian government for help concerning Scatarie Island. *"It is usually the first land made by vessels from Europe to any of the colonies eastward of the Bay of Fundy,"* he wrote, *"the first news of its propinquity being often given by the roar of breakers or the concussion of its rocks. Shipwrecks are of frequent occurrence there, and few places on the coast of Northern America more obviously call for the precaution of a lighthouse."*

Haliburton's words fell on deaf ears, but two years later, Canadians were listening; for the name Scatarie was prominent in the news: The troopship LEONIDAS, *"conveying troops and a large amount of specie to the military chest in Canada was wrecked on the island of Scatarie and totally lost,"* so reported the Times. All the British soldiers perished, plus a fortune in British coins. It was such an overwhelming disaster that the fishermen of nearby Main-a-Dieu were convinced that a Humane Society rescue station and a lighthouse would be built and manned immediately, but this didn't happen, and the villagers were happy, for they didn't want a lighthouse on their island. Scatarie was not only their offshore fishing station in the summer, but their provider of goods, sometimes luxuries and treasures from shipwrecks in the winters.

In the following year, 1833, two immigrant vessels hit the island. The VOL-UNTEER carrying 255 persons to Quebec from Britain, and the HOPE, with 145 immigrants. Most were saved and brought to Main-a-Dieu where they remained for weeks to be fed and housed by villagers until rescue ships came from Sydney, Cape Breton's capital, and from Halifax. The villagers now were the destitute ones, their laders cleaned out by the hungry immigrants. Many presented the provincial government with hefty food bills, but no recompense was forthcoming. The people of Sydney, some 20 miles northwest, were also shackled with added expense feeding and treating shipwreck victims, also without compensation from the government. The following year, the Canadian House was hit with what they called an "exorbitant bill" of 26,306 pounds sterling for the *"rescuing of stranded mariners from eight vessels near Scatarie Island,"* This was the year that troubles at Scatarie almost broke the Canadian bank and forced the government into action. There were ten major shipwrecks at the island that winter of 1834. On one ship, the ASTREA, 251 Irish immigrants drowned, many were stranded and some died of exposure or hunger on the island. But, 406 people from the nine other ships were saved, fed and treated for frostbite and wounds at Main-a-Dieu, but reluctantly. The villagers were screaming for compensation for their depleted food supplies and constant inconvenience in their homes for having to accommodate shipwreck victims.

The worst of the ten 1834 disasters at the island was the grounding of the brig FIDELITY with 183 immigrants from Dublin, Ireland aboard. All rejoiced at reaching the island safely, but their thankful prayers of deliverance were soon moans and groans of suffering, for there was no food or shelter on the island, except for a few dead fish that washed ashore and two tiny fisherman huts. Because ice-flows blocked the channel to the mainland, help didn't come for days, during which time, four people froze to death, even though it was early spring. Then, when Main-a-Dieu fishermen began to row people ashore from the island, a few at a time, the village homes were soon filled to the rafters and the villagers ran out of food. A messenger was sent to Sydney, begging for relief, but by the time rescue boats arrived, the villagers were destitute and resentful. They decided to attack the abandoned FIDELITY and rob it of every item aboard, including personal possessions, the captain's safe and all nautical equipment and fittings. All valuables, including a sizable amount of coins, were taken and buried on the island to be dug up later – Scatarie becoming an offshore bank for the fishermen. Government officials from Halifax and Sydney were shocked at the thieving of the villagers, but the men of Main-a-Dieu felt completely justified at cleaning out the FIDELITY, to compensate for their food losses and reward for saving so many immigrants. In fact, while robbing the stranded brig, they discovered two women and a girl who were still living on the island and near starvation. They were passengers of the FIDELI-TY, who surely would have died had the village fishermen not returned to pirate the wreck. It was soon after this incident that Sam Cunard, the lighthouse commissioner of the Maritimes, partitioned the Canadian government to build a lighthouse at Scatarie Island, "without delay." Cunard was the most influential man in Nova Scotia and Cape Breton and the funds were immediately provided for the building of a lighthouse at this hazardous island, prompted it seems, not because of ruined vessels and distressed passengers, but because the villagers of Main-a-Dieu had taken up wrecking.

Even a greater threat to shipping and life and limb to mariners in the freezing North Atlantic, is the island of St. Paul, some eighty miles north of Scatarie, and but ten miles off the northern tip of Cape Breton. Although only three miles long and a mile wide, it is possibly the most treacherous little outcropping of land in the Atlantic. For it is here that the Labrador Current meets the waters of the St. Lawrence River and foam along the terrible high cliffs facing the Atlantic and the Cabot Strait. It has long been called the "Graveyard of the Gulf." The constant mix of cold and warm waters off the island causes an almost permanent fog, and an undetected error in the British navigational charts of the early 1800s, made the area even more treacherous. Being the entrance to the Gulf of Saint Lawrence, the waters were and still are frequently traveled and St. Paul Island has devastated many a vessel. Adding to the horror of shipwreck was that the island shoreline cliffs rise to over 400-feet in height, *"and they are nearly perpendicular,"* wrote engineer John Adams, the man chosen to build a lighthouse there in 1837. At the base of a cliff, before he built the lighthouse, Adams found a fistful of gold Spanish coins in a seaside crevice, which was one of the reasons the island was so popular with wreckers.

Apparently many Spanish vessels frequented this area in the 16th and 17th centuries, possibly following the Gulf Stream or sailing north to purchase dried and salted cod from the Bretons before traveling home to Spain. Many Spanish galleons foundered at St. Paul, depositing gold, silver and emeralds from Central America there. Being so close to the mainland, the wreckers here, like on Scatarie Island, took on the guise of fishermen and seal hunters. They would frequent the island before the ice melted and be first to find the remains of ships and cargoes that never made home port over the winter. Stripping wreckage and frozen corpses became quite lucrative for the sealers prior to the coming of Adam's two lighthouses, which were built on the Northwest and Southeast coasts of the island respectively. Getting the lighthouses built, however, was not only a physically exhausting enterprise, but a political one as well. Two Canadian provinces claimed the little island, and neither seemed willing to yield custody of the island to the other, which almost ended in an all out war between the two claimants.

A Scotsman named McKenzie, with two other Cape Bretons went to St. Paul to live in 1832, surviving on fishing, sealing and wrecking. They built huts on the east end of the island at what is called Atlantic Cove, and food was supplied to them from the provincial government of Nova Scotia, in return for them to oversee wrecks, salvage and possibly save lives of shipwreck victims. Unbeknownst to McKenzie and his men, the provincial government of New Brunswick had decided to also place men permanently on this treacherous little island over the winter of 1832, and they built their wrecker-rescue station on the west end of the island at Trinity Cove. The New Brunswick men, Wigmore and White, were also there to *"aid vessels which may wreck along the shores of the island."* The possibilities of salvaging valuable cargoes for both crews was very good, and profits for the two provincial governments were expected, for the island produced an average of five major shipwrecks per year. The brisk business began on the west end of the island near Trinity Cove, when in early December, the ship GREAT BRITAIN grounded in a snowstorm. Before White and Wigmore got to the ship, she had begun to break apart, and only four of her thirty-man crew reached shore alive. One survivor, not seeing the New Brunswick station, walked across the island and came upon McKenzie's hut on the eastside. McKenzie and his men treated and fed the half-frozen crewmen, then following his tracks in the snow, walked to the west-end of the island looking for survivors and, of course, any loot they could salvage. Instead, they bumped into White and Wigmore at the wreck site. Both teams were surprised that they had been living at opposite sides of the island for weeks without knowing the other was there. Although their missions were the same, and they both represented the British-Canadian government, they were at cross-purposes. The New Brunswick men were not about to allow McKenzie to loot their newfound wreck. McKenzie told them that Nova Scotia hadn't sent their supply ship and he and his men were low on supplies, could the New Brunswick team share some of their food? The answer was "No," and the atmosphere between the two wrecking-rescue teams became as frigid as the weather. To add insult to injury, White and Wigmore wanted the wreck survivor that McKenzie held in his hut, for the survivors that the New Brunswick team had treated died of frostbite at their station. McKenzie wouldn't release the survivor to them, nor did the shipwreck survivor want to go into the New Brunswick camp, after he discovered that his crewmates had died under their care. Animosities between the two teams grew, until McKenzie and his team, with their patient, were forced to sail for the mainland in early January because they had no food left. A storm sent their little vessel out to sea and they were lost for four days, finally landing at Ingoish, all aboard almost frozen and starved to death. McKenzie blamed the New Brunswick men for his dilemma. Around the same time, White also attempted to row the ten miles to the mainland, lost an oar during his attempt and drifted out to sea, only to be picked up three days later by a British ship whose skipper refused to turn back to Canada. He deposited White of the New Brunswick team in England. *" 'Tis only justice from above,"* McKenzie commented when he heard of White's unplanned voyage.

White didn't return to St. Paul Island, but the New Brunswick authorities replaced him with Donald Moon. Apparently Mr. Moon had some political clout, for when the first lighthouse was built on the island, he became the first lighthouse keeper, and not Cape Breton's McKenzie. Moon, however, shortly thereafter lost his life on the island, trying to save shipwreck victims. He left the lighthouse to save seal fishermen who were caught in the icepacks off shore, and neither he nor the fishermen were seen again. According to John Campbell's Journal, *"it was the night of a fierce gale,"* and, *"for seven days and nights, no one came to the lighthouse. It was out of their power to reach it, and during those nights, Mrs. Moon, save for the baby at her breast, was alone in her terrible grief, yet she kept the light burning."* It was John Campbell who came to the lighthouse on the eighth day and comforted the distraught woman. It was also Campbell who was later made superintendent of the island for 18 years that fought for Mrs. Moon's rights with the Canadian government. The government authorities had refused to give the lighthouse keeper's widow and their child a pension, which stemmed from earlier conflicts between the provinces over St. Paul Island. Campbell managed to ease the political fury between the province politicians. And, not only he, but his son and grandson became superintendents and lighthouse keepers on St. Paul, stretching over a period of 82 years.

A year after the McKenzie-White disagreement over food supplies and the GREAT-BRITAIN survivor, five vessels hit the high cliffs of St. Paul, with a loss of some 200 lives, four of them sinking in one night. One of them that struck was the MARGARET from Dublin with 300 immigrants aboard, but miraculously there was no loss of life from the MARGARET. The lighthouses were erected two years later, and although John Adams, the builder, wanted only one light at the top of the island at Beacon Hill, the governments wisely decided on two, to appease the two provinces, one at either end of the island. Once they were built, the wreckers left the island, and there were no ship-wrecks at St. Paul Island for six years.

At Jessie Cove, where the Southwest Lighthouse stands today at St. Paul, is the site of probably the island's most memorable disaster; memorable, not for the shipwreck itself, but for the aftermath, which brought to light the true mission of many seal hunters of the North Atlantic. The barque JESSIE, sailing from Prince Edward Island on the day before Christmas, 1824, encountered a fierce snowstorm in the Cabot Straits on New Years Day and smashed into the jagged cliffs of St. Paul. There were 28 persons on board and they all made it safely to shore under the leadership of the barque owner, Donal MacKay, but their vessel was a total wreck and soon sank. They made huts of driftwood and large bonfires, hoping to signal the people on the mainland only some ten miles away, but no one saw their fires, and if they did, they didn't come. Ice-flow and pack-ice would make rescue impossible anyway, for no rowboat or sailing ship could make it through the icy chowder with its sharp icebergs and swift currents. Donal MacKay kept a journal revealing the day to day suffering of the shipwreck victims and how they died off one by one of starvation and exposure, until his last entry on March 17, 1825, when he dropped his pen for good. Loved ones back at Prince Edward Island, however, received no word of the fate of the JESSIE. Over a year went by and still there was no word. Alice MacKay, Donal's wife expected the worst, for the barque had not been reported entering any port, but she hoped beyond hope that her husband might still be alive. One can only imagine her initial shock one morning at the general store in Charlottetown, when she spied her husband standing at the shop counter. It was his hat and his coat, but when she approached the man, her body trembling with anticipation, she sighed with grief, for it was not him. The coat, however, she knew was Donal's, for she had made it specially for him. She immediately confronted the man and boldly pulled open the coat, and pointed to the initials 'D.M.' which she had sewn into the lining. The man, wide-eyed and obviously frightened, pulled away from Mrs. MacKay and ran out of the store and up the street, with her right behind him, shouting *"murderer, murderer. This man murdered my husband!"* The man was finally tackled and held down by bystanders who knew Mrs. MacKay, and they soon forced a confession out of him. He had found a body wrapped in the coat while he was seal hunting at St. Paul Island. Soon the man was carried off to the authorities, where further information was forced out of him. The body of Donal MacKay had also carried his diary and over 100 gold guineas, some of which the seal hunter had spent. Every item was returned to Mrs. MacKay, and the thieving hunter went away for a few years to a Canadian prison. Mrs. MacKay went to St. Paul with assistants and found all of the corpses, which were returned to Prince Edward Island for proper burial. The other thieving seal hunters, their identities revealed by the coat robber, were hunted down, brought to trial, convicted and all served jail sentences – and thus the age of the wreckers slowly dimmed as fate and the wonderful glow of the lighthouses exposed their treacheries. They are no more.

Bakers Island Light in Salem's outer harbor.

The Lighthouse At Bishop Rock, Scilly, Isles, England, built in 1851.

The 270-foot City Of Columbus strikes Devil's Bridge, off Martha's Vineyard, Massachusetts, January 18, 1884.
Sketch from Harper's Weekly Magazine

On the morning after the wreck of City Of Columbus, Gay Head Light stands as sole sentry over Devil's Bridge.
Photo courtesy Peabody-Essex Museum, Salem, MA.

Peter Johnson, one of the Gay Head Indians who rescued survivors from the City Of Columbus, was later featured at the Austin & Stone Museum in Boston. A few years later he was murdered.
Photo courtesy Peabody-Essex Museum, Salem, MA.

Gay Head Light, Martha's Vineyard – the scene of murder and tragic ship-wrecks.
U.S. Coast Guard photo.

Chapter 2
Disaster At Devil's Bridge

One of the most breathtaking wonders of Massachusetts is Gay Head on the western shore of Martha's Vineyard Island off Cape Cod. Colorful clay cliffs tower 150 feet above the sea overlooking Vineyard Sound. Red, yellow, purple, brown, green and white bluffs of what looks like playdough cover some 6,000 feet of surface area, splashed over sand and rocks like some abstract painting, and above it all stands a brownstone lighthouse – the lone candle on a multicolored cake of clay.

Living near the lighthouse is a small colony of Indians. They use the clay of Gay Head to make pottery, as did their ancestors many centuries before the first lighthouse was built there in 1798. These Indians of the Wampanoag Nation, noted for their interaction with the Pilgrims in 1620, were also outstanding whalers and unrelenting toilers of the sea in the 18th and 19th centuries. Even today, their boats are always ready, stored at the foot of Gay Head or tucked into nearby inlets, to board in an effort to save shipwreck victims and to collect wood from ill-fated ships. Wood to burn or build has always been hard to come by at wind-swept Gay Head, but shipwrecks, especially in winter, were once fairly frequent and provided fuel for the campfires. Vineyard Sound has been the watery highway to and from Boston, south and east, since Colonial times, but lurking just below the surface waters in this tidal strait is a one mile square sunken shoal called Devil's Bridge. It has destroyed many a vessel, but local mariners are wary of the sunken rock bridge and give it a wide berth, sailing or cruising close to the Elizabeth Islands, some four miles distant from the Vineyard. Devil's Bridge has long been well marked by a buoy, and, of course, distinguished at night by Gay Head Light.

The first keeper of the wooden lighthouse, Ebenezer Skiff, was constantly complaining to the President of the United States about conditions at Gay Head. First was about bits of colored clay splattering the glass of the light during storms, a unique problem not endured by other lighthouse keepers, and he needed more money to deal with it. Indians, probably the same ones Skiff hired to clean the windows of clay, were stealing his wood, and collected all driftwood that came ashore before he could get to it. One of his letters reads as follows: *"Sir, clay and oker of different colours from which this place derived its name ascend in a sheet of wind pened by the high cliffs and catch on the lighthouse glass, which often requires cleaning on the outside – tedious service in cold weather, and additional to what is necessary in any other part of Massachusetts.*

"The spring of water in the edge of the cliff is not sufficient, and rain colors the water to blood. I cart the water used by my family more than half a mile. It

is necessary to keep a draught horse and carriage for that purpose and frequently I have to travel in a hilly common extending five miles to find the horse.

"My firewood is brought from the mainland and, there being neither harbor nor wharf here, it is more expensive than in seaports. Keepers in some places get their wood with little cost; but here the native Indians watch the shores to take all drifts.

"It is about eight miles from here to a gristmill and in the common way of passing are creeks not fordable at all seasons. The business respecting the light is, mostly done by me in person, yet I occasionally leave home to procure wood and many other necessaries; previous to which I have to agree with and instruct some trusty white person to tend the light in my absence: if my salary would admit, I would hire some person to live constantly with me lest I should be sick – I have no neighbors here but Indians or people of colour...

"When I hire an Indian to work I usually give him a dollar per day when the days are long and seventy five cents a day when the days are short, and I give him three meals worth twenty-five cents each, amounting to seventy-five cents, which is seven cents more than the wages for my services both day and night (while I board myself) only sixty-eight cents, computing my salary (as it is now) of two hundred and fifty dollars a year, and the year to consist of three hundred and sixty five days. . . I humbly pray you to take this matter into your wise consideration and afford me relief by granting an increase to my salary. I am Sir, with all possibly respect, yours to command, Ebenezer Skiff "

President Jefferson approved a fifty dollar increase to Skiff in 1805, and he received fifty dollars more per year when he sent the same letter, almost verbatim, to President Madison ten years later. It was in 1823, however, that Keeper Skiff had much more to complain about, for early that year, he had a murder on his hands.

A February storm had carried the brig PILGRIM across Devil's Bridge, splintering her bottom and dumping her mahogany logs cargo at the foot of Gay Head. The Indians swooped down on the logs and began carrying them home, which infuriated Keeper Skiff, for he could find no one to help him collect a pile of logs for himself, and they were too big and cumbersome for one man to carry. The greatest collection of logs from the PILGRIM were confiscated by an Indian woman, Mary Cuff, only recently with child. She would persuade men, including her husband, to take one end of a log, as she struggled with the other in carrying it up the steep cliffs to her house, then she would return to the beach for another, and continue throughout the day, day after day, when the Indian men had long before quit from exhaustion. One of her helpers was Richard Johnson, a New York black man, who had only been on the island for three years, but lived with Mary's old father-in-law, Jonathan Cuff. Johnson told Jonathon that Mary Cuff's child was his. Johnson was strong and almost as energetic as Mary, but insisted that half the logs they carried up the cliffs should belong to him. Mary thought differently, and felt that two thirds of the logs retrieved should be hers, for she was first to spot the wreck and claim the cargo. Keeper Skiff witnessed their argument over the logs from his station atop the cliffs, but thought little of it, for the local Indians argued and bickered among themselves quite frequently.

A week after the wreck, in the early morning of March 2nd, as Keeper Skiff climbed the winding stairs to snuff the whaleoil lantern, he spotted Mary Cuff, heading down the clay cliffs, apparently after the remaining few logs that were on the beach. She had left her baby at home in the care of her husband. Skiff thought it strange that there was no man with her to help carry up the logs, but Skiff surmised that she had probably worn them all out. A few moments later, Skiff heard a terrifying scream come from the base of the cliffs, and then the harsh shouting of a man, but the lighthouse keeper thought little more about it – just Mary screaming at one of her over-worked male helpers, thought Skiff, and he continued on with his duties in the tower. Later that day it grew bitterly cold and began to snow. The skies darkened and Skiff lit the lamp early. Next morning, Skiff saw Indian woman Jane Wanley descend the cliffs, and a few minutes later, he heard another terrifying scream. This time, Skiff left the lighthouse, to be greeted by Jane Wanley, shouting as she climbed the cliffs towards him, *"Mary Cuff is dead on the sand below. Her head's bashed in."* Jane was sobbing hysterically, and Skiff brought her into his house. He then rode his horse into Vineyard Haven for the Sheriff. The Indian community, which numbered less than 160 people, was angry and frightened. There was a murderer in their midst, and almost to a man, they were convinced it was Richard Johnson, the New Yorker. David Cuff, Mary's husband, was also a suspect, however, for he had allowed almost two days to expire before he told anyone that his wife was missing. A neighboring family of Indians testified that they had found a bloodied club near the Cuff house, but burned it in their fire, for the need for wood was so vital on such cold nights. Without any evidence, but on the insistence of the Indians, the Sheriff arrested Richard Johnson.

The trial was on the mainland at Barnstable Court, Cape Cod, on July 8, 1829 and a schooner chartered by the state was sent to Martha's Vineyard to transport the prisoner, Sheriff, two deputies, Mary Cuff's family, and all witnesses, including Keeper Skiff. It was the first time in 24 years that Keeper Skiff had been to the mainland, and the first time in history that the running of a lighthouse was turned over to an Indian while Skiff was gone. It wasn't until the 20th century that Gay Head Indians actually took over the running of their own lighthouse.

Keeper Skiff testified about hearing Mary scream from below the cliff on the morning of the murder, and that he had heard an angry man's voice, but he couldn't identify it as Richard Johnson's voice. Two Indian girls testified that they saw Richard Johnson and Mary Cuff fighting on the cliffs that morning, but their testimonies were stricken from the record, for the girls were known as notorious liars. The jury found Richard Johnson innocent, and needless to say, he didn't return on the schooner that ferried the angry islanders back to the Vineyard after the trial. In fact, Johnson disappeared for five years, when again he was accused of murdering a woman, this time in New York City. Johnson was found guilty of shooting Ursula Newman and was later hanged. Justice finally prevailed, but poor old Ebenezer Skiff was never forgiven by the Indian community of Gay Head for not investigating the screams of Mary Cuff on the morning of her murder, and it was said by others at the time that he never forgave himself either.

It was nineteen years after the murder, long after Keeper Skiff had permanently retired to the mainland, that it was decided to tear down the old wooden lighthouse and build a replacement of brick and steel. Lighthouse inspector I. P. Lewis, in 1842, reported that Gay Head Light was *"very deficient in power, and at a distance of twelve miles is obscured about three-fourths of the time."* He recommended a *"first-order light that can be seen at a distance of from nineteen to twenty miles."* The authorities adopted Lewis' recommendation, but the lighthouse wasn't constructed until fourteen more years had elapsed. It still stands today, towering 51 feet above the cliffs, painted red, with every fourth flash a red flash, to be seen twenty miles to sea. It was 28 years later, almost to the day that the new light was installed and working, that, as <u>Harper's Weekly</u> reported, *"there was a disaster, so sudden, so terrible and so complete that it shocked the country as no like disaster has in years."*

It was four a.m. on the cold frosty morning of January 18, 1884, when Nathanial Bunker, in bed at his home in New Market, New Hampshire, woke from a nightmare, screaming. He had dreamed that he was standing on a high colorful cliff beside a lighthouse, *"and I was looking down on a large steamship as it hit a reef and began to sink. I could see men, women and children all struggling in the water,"* Bunker told two friends early that morning. *"Wreckage was everywhere,"* he reported, *"and I saw Lou Chase trying to help my daughter into a lifeboat, but a big wave came and swept everything away."* Bunker's two friends had found the old man screaming and sobbing in bed, and although they knew that his daughter and Lou Chase had just married and were honeymooning aboard the steamer CITY OF COLUMBUS, they assured Bunker that it was only a bad dream. *"I know I'll never see them again,"* cried Bunker, and he was right, for the news came to New Market, New Hampshire that night that the great steamer CITY OF COLUMBUS had sunk at about the time Bunker was having his nightmare. She had struck Devil's Bridge, and down with her went 103 who were aboard, including Nathanial Bunker's daughter and his new son-in-law. The Boston Evening Transcript called the CITY OF COLUMBUS a *"floating palace."*

She was steeped in luxury, but also carried cargo to and from Boston and Georgia, mostly cotton and potatoes, and she'd usually make the trip in six days. She was 2,000 tons and 270 feet long, carrying 132 people on her final voyage, heading for the warmth of Savannah. The sea was spitting and the wind was up, as the steamer entered Vineyard Sound in the wee hours of the morning. Captain Schuyler Wright turned over the helm and pilot house to second officer Harding, and retired to his room behind the pilot house to get warm by the heater and to chew tobacco. He sat dozing for over an hour, when he heard watchman Leary cry, *"Buoy on port bow!"* Captain Wright knew that the only buoy in the vicinity marked Devil's Bridge. Wright raced for the pilot-house as the helmsman spun the wheel to port. Towering above them, just over half a mile away, was Gay Head Light. The CITY OF COLUMBUS was off course and she smashed into Devil's Bridge with a mighty impact, which some said sounded like the *"roar of a cannon. "*

Captain Wright ordered the engineer to back the steamer off the rocks, putting her into deep water. If she had remained on the rocks, she would have sunk to 15 feet and remained mostly above water, possibly saving everyone aboard. The rigging of the ship did remain above the sea when she sank, and some thirty passengers and crew sought shelter there, but most were found a few hours later, frozen solid to the shrouds and lines. The steamer remained afloat only eight minutes from the moment she hit Devil's Bridge.

Ship's Purser Spaulding, who was one of the first into the rigging as the sea raged about him, said that, *"Men and women, some with children in their arms, clambered up the deck, clinging frantically to every projection that offered assistance. They crowded upon each other so fast they could not be counted as they rushed out on deck, only to be met by waves and swept into the sea. Groans, yells and curses mingled with the gale. Women shrieked and men shouted. Men and women clutched each other regardlessly, all the while struggling against each other in the frenzied attempt to save themselves."*

Seaman John White later reported that *"I saw some women rush on deck with their husbands, and the full force of the storm broke upon them, realizing all was lost, they threw their arms around their husbands' necks. A few moments later they were swept overboard. It was fearful the way the women were swept away. A mother with her child held tightly in her arms, was borne away almost as she reached the deck. Not one woman reached the rigging."* Survivor John Cook added that, *"All deference to sex seemed lost in the struggle to reach the few available places of safety,"* but Cook also said he saw a man and a woman standing close together, *"hand in hand, unmoved by the turmoil about them. Spray was drenching them as the man leaned over and kissed the woman. They were embracing,"* Cook reported, *"when a heavy sea washed them away."*

Possibly the newlyweds, Lou Chase and Sally Bunker Chase from New Market, New Hampshire.

As foaming seas reached the main-deck, *"a massive wave encompassed the steamer,"* testified Captain Wright at a later hearing, *"and a great cry of terror reached ears aloft. The deck disappeared under curling, foaming eddies... Then all were gone and the only sounds were those of whipping gale and dashing seas. For an instant it was deathly still, but those shrieks were in my ears. 'Help! help! help!' but I could give no help. It was all over, except for the few of us in the masts and rigging."* High in the rigging was passenger Fred Tibbetts. He wasn't cold and he wasn't wet. He wore a heavy coat and a life-vest, and had leaped into the rigging before the deck was awash and climbed high enough to avoid the cold salt spray that turned to ice as it splashed the survivors clutching for dear life below him. *"Just beneath us, in plain sight and out of reach, were those poor doomed creatures,"* he later recounted. In the crowded rigging, Tibbetts tried to lift the spirits of his friend Frank May, who held onto the icy rope with one hand, and squeezed Fred's hand with the other. *"Cheer up,"* Tibbetts shouted to all around him, and pointing to the lighthouse, he cried through the wind, *"Boys, we'll be having a New England breakfast up there."* Yet, as the bright light continued to circle, bathing the survivors in its beam, there seemed to be no activity on shore, no rescue boats heading out for them to attempt to save them. They had to wait over an hour, almost until dawn, before they were spotted, and in that precious time, many in the rigging fell off into the sea, or like Frank May, just bowed his head in death, but continued to cling, his clothes frozen to the rigging.

In the Gay Head Lighthouse, some 200 feet above the surf, Assistant Keeper Fred Poole spied a light on the surface of Devil's Bridge at about five a.m. He watched for a few minutes, and when the light did not move, he woke up Keeper Horatio Pease, who had been the chief at the light for over twenty years. Pease had never seen anything like it, but rightly concluded it was a shipwreck on Devil's Bridge. The Humane Society had recently purchased lifeboats for the Gay Head Indians, to be kept near the Indian Village landing for the purpose of shipwreck rescue. Pease spread the alarm, and as the sun rose and the plight of survivors in the rigging became evident to the keeper and his assistant, they began waving a blanket from the lighthouse balcony, to assure the victims that they had been spotted and that help was on the way. There were six Indian whalers to a boat, and two boats were launched into the heavy surf, one immediately capsizing, but all rescuers were saved, and wearing wet clothes, they also succeeded to launch boat-two into and over the breakers. Joseph Peters was in charge of boat-one and James Mosher of boat two. As they struggled to get to the wreck-site, a steamer headed up the Sound, the GLAUCUS out of Boston. *"Here's our rescue,"* Tibbetts shouted to the others in the rigging, but the steamer passed them by. Three officers of the

GLAUCUS, including her captain, Maynard Bearse, when confronted later by authorities and the press, for not stopping to save the men in the rigging, all stated that they saw no people in the rigging. It was fairly dark, near dawn and the seas were rough so they didn't venture too close to the wreck, but it seems almost impossible, as it did to many then, that the officers on deck aboard the GLAUCUS never saw the thirty or more men clinging for life in the rigging of the CITY OF COLUMBUS.

It took the Indians in boat-one over one hour to row to the wreck site through heavy swells and a multitude of flotsam, including dead bodies and pieces of the ship that were being spewed up from her sunken tomb. *"Boys, the lifeboat is here,"* cried Tibbetts with glee, *"and such a shout went up over the waters from the rigging, but I doubt if we could be heard, for when the lifeboat was not more than fifty yards from us, not a sound reached our ears from the men in the boat. We only at last made out by the motions of the man in the bow that he wanted us to jump and swim to them."*

Five members of the crew jumped into the cold frothing sea and safely reached the lifeboat. *"I was determined to try for it,"* said Tibbetts later, *"but I was too high to jump. It was also impossible to pass the men in the rigging below me. My only chance was to attempt going down on the underside of the rigging, clinging to the ratlines. I did it. When about half way down a big, burly man just over me glared at me like a maniac, shook his clenched fist in my face and shouted: 'Don't you dare go to that boat before me.' I got away from him as quickly as possible and was soon down close to the tumbling waters. Beside me I found Purser Spaulding. He kindly explained to me how to take advantage of the receding breakers in swimming to the boat. Suddenly those in the rigging cried, 'Look out! A breaker!' On came an avalanche of water. It nearly buried me. As the wave receded I thought, 'It's time to go.' I let go the ratline and jumped. As I began to swim for the boat, another sea caught me and rolled me over. When I could breathe again, I found myself headed for the lifeboat. A boathook was thrust under my arm and two grips caught my shoulders, and over the gunwale I came. I seized an oar and began to work with the others to keep from freezing. Immediately after me came the purser. They hauled him in, and the boat having all it could carry, signaled for no more to leave the wreck. We started on a roundabout pull for Gay Head wharf. There were seven of us saved from the wreck, six of the steamer's company and one passenger – myself."*

As the six Indians in boat-two struggled to get to the wreck, a few of those hanging in the rigging could hold on no longer and they fell into the icy sea and were swallowed by it. *"I saw waiter Bill Boardman fall into the sea,"* reported crewman Furber Hanson, *"after the first lifeboat headed back to shore. He was so cold he didn't make a struggle. In a moment I looked again and he was gone."* At the same time, the CITY OF COLUMBUS smokestack was ripped from the ship by the pounding of breakers and fell into the rigging, sweeping passenger Fred Sargent from his perch and dragging him under. The mass of debris now floating in the water made it difficult for the Indians to maneuver their rowboat under the fifteen or so shipwreck victims who vainly held on for dear life and hopeful rescue. James Mosher followed the same procedure as the skipper of boat-one and shouted for the survivors to leap from the rigging into the cold swirling water. Reluctant at first, only because they were shivering from cold and dreaded the icy sea, all but eight men jumped and swam to the lifeboat to be hauled aboard. The eight left in the rigging refused to jump, or as Mosher and his men assumed, were possibly unconscious or dead. To save his few passengers from freezing to death, Mosher ordered his men to row back to Gay Head wharf. In all, the courageous Gay Head Indians saved seventeen men from the wreck at Devil's Bridge. No women and only one 12-year-old child, George Farnsworth, survived. Thirty two women and seven children drowned.

The Revenue Cutter DEXTER was soon on the scene. *"A gale had been steadily rising,"* reported her captain, Eric Gabrielson. *"The sea was blowing very hard, and the sea rolled mountain high."* With much difficulty, the DEXTER anchored off the wreck at Devil's Bridge, and Lieutenant John Rhodes volunteered with five seamen to row in the DEXTER longboat to place themselves under the rigging. Rhodes swam to the mast and climbed the rigging to help some make the plunge into the sea. Others, he all but carried to the bobbing rescue boat. In all, Rhodes and his men rescued seven, two of whom died once aboard the DEXTER. Five of the CITY OF COLUMBUS crewmen managed to ride in a semi-submerged longboat to shore, but otherwise there were no survivors. Of the 87 passengers, 75 died, and only 17 of the 45 officers and crew survived. Most of the bodies drifted ashore to the foot of the clay cliffs of Gay Head, along with other wreckage and cargo. Indian women scoured the beach for wood and potatoes and shoes. One Indian filled his boat so full of potatoes he had no room to bring lifeless shipwreck victims aboard, and he was highly criticized by authorities. Most bodies were brought into New Bedford and were laid out in frozen form at a local barn for friends and relatives to identify. Many bodies and some twelve survivors, however, could not be transported to the mainland from Martha's Vineyard, because of a great blizzard that swept the island the day after the shipwreck. Friends and families of these few survivors had concluded that their loved ones went down with the ship, but they experienced a miraculous surprise a few days later when news reporters ventured to the island and found survivors being warmly cared for by Indians in their humble dwellings and by Keeper Horatio Pease, high up in the lantern room of the Gay Head Lighthouse. Captain Schuyler Wright was one who survived, but told others that he wished he hadn't. He, of course, lost his captain's license, and he lived out the remainder of his life as a dock worker in Savannah, Georgia.

Lieutenant John Rhodes received great acclaim for his bravery, as did the twelve Gay Head Indians who manned the lifeboats. They also split a $3,500 reward donated from various newspapers for their valor. One of the recipients was oarsman in boat-two, Peter Johnson. He received $160, one of the top grants, plus a silver medal. He then went on to be featured at a Boston museum, carrying an oar on stage as he told of his part in the rescue at Devil's Bridge, making $100 per week – big money in those days. Seven years after the CITY OF COLUMBUS disaster, the body of Peter Johnson was found on Egg Island near Vineyard Sound – he had been murdered, his head bashed in by a rock. Could this Peter Johnson of Gay Head be a descendant of Richard Johnson, the black man who murdered Indian Mary Cuff back in 1823? Peter was a mixture of Indian and African, one of a minority of mixed race living with the 100 or more Indians at Gay Head. Peter Johnson could well have been the child Mary Cuff delivered only weeks before the murder – the child Richard Johnson insisted he fathered. *"The sins of the father shall be visited upon his children."* And so, Biblical prophecy may be quite fitting concerning those years of mayhem and great tragedy, all performed under the light before America's most colorful and treacherous of backdrops, the clay cliffs of Gay Head.

Cape Hatteras Lighthouse in North Carolina, also known as "Hamilton's Light," is 193-feet high, the tallest lighthouse in America.
U.S. Coast Guard photo.

Portrait of Theodosia Burr Alston, by John Vanderlyn, survived the
sinking of the schooner PATRIOT by wreckers in January, 1813, and
was later recovered in a wrecker's shack at Nag's Head.
Photo courtesy the New York Historical Society.
Insert is portrait of Aaron Burr, also painted by John Vanderlyn in 1802.

Chapter 3
Curse Of The Burrs

Probably one of the best-loved men in American history was Alexander Hamilton. He was born illegitimate in 1755 at Nevis in the West Indies, and spent a carefree youth on Saint Croix, but at age 18 he was sent to what is now Columbia University, New York, for some serious study. He was a brilliant student, and while in college, then called King's College, he wrote many influential anti-British pamphlets, condemning the English king and parliament. When the spark of Revolution was ignited at Lexington and Concord, he was commissioned a captain in the New York artillery. It wasn't long before General George Washington recognized Hamilton as a military genius, and he made Alexander his personal aide-de-camp. After the war he returned to college and obtained a law degree and was admitted to the bar in New York state. His constant activity in community affairs, and his ever-increasing love for politics, prompted him to be chosen as a delegate to the Constitutional Convention at Philadelphia in 1787. To gain approval from the citizens of New York, he, with James Madison and John Jay, wrote 85 essays for the New York newspapers on the structure and ingredients of the proposed American Constitution, which became a political classic known as *"The Federalist Papers."* President George Washington chose Hamilton to serve as America's first Secretary of the Treasury, and at age 33, he became leader of the Federalist Party.

It was inevitable that such a bright burning star in American politics would have an equally capable nemesis – he was the turbulent, ever ruthless Aaron Burr. Only a year younger than Hamilton, Burr was from a prominent New Jersey family, and also a New York lawyer. Like Hamilton, he served on General George Washington's staff during the Revolution, but he got on Washington's nerves, so George transferred him out to another unit. Burr also became somewhat suspect when he married Theodosia Prevost, widow of a British army officer. The Burrs soon became noted for their lavish social-political parties, and after being elected to the New York assembly, Burr was appointed attorney general in 1789. Within two years he built a strong political machine that defeated General Philip Schuyler, winning him a seat in the United States Senate. Schuyler considered Burr his lifelong enemy, as did the General's son-in-law, Alexander Hamilton. It was the beginning of a feud that would end in death and destruction.

Aaron Burr was on the presidential ticket in the year 1800, along with Virginian Thomas Jefferson, and because Burr carried New York, their ticket won the election. In those days, however, the voters elected the party ticket and not either man for president or vice-president. By majority vote, the House of Representatives would decide which man would be President. When the votes were counted, both men had seventy-three – it was a tie, and after balloting 35 more times, it still remained a tie. It was Matthew Lyons, Congressman from Vermont, persuaded by Alexander Hamilton, who changed his vote on the 36th ballot and voted for Thomas Jefferson, thus making him the third President of the United States, and Aaron Burr, the third Vice-President. Burr was not too happy with Hamilton. He had further reason to hate Hamilton when, four years later, Burr was nominated to be Governor of New York by the state legislature, only to be thwarted once again by the influence of Hamilton and his friends, who saw to it that Burr did not become Governor Adding insult to injury, Hamilton assisted George Clinton in replacing Burr as the vice-presidential candidate on the Republican ticket. Burr demanded an explanation from Hamilton as to why he was constantly denigrating his character. Not receiving a satisfactory response, he goaded Hamilton into a duel. Duels were, of course, legal then, although many found them repulsive. Hamilton, in fact, didn't seem to take Burr's challenge seriously, and postponed the dates of the encounter three times. Burr was angry and insistent. His honor had been slandered, and Hamilton finally felt obliged to meet him on the *"field of honor"* at an open field in Weehawken, New Jersey at the break of day on July 11, 1804. Each faced the other, aimed and fired. Hamilton's shot missed, but Burr's hit the mark and Hamilton was killed. The public was outraged, and Burr now had a host of enemies, all out to do him harm.

To avoid the wrath of Hamilton's friends, Burr headed West, but it wasn't long before his seemingly sordid ambitions got him into deep trouble and provided means for retribution by Hamilton lovers, which included President Thomas Jefferson. Colonel Aaron Burr attempted to have Kentucky, Tennessee and the Mississippi Territory secede from the Union to begin a new and separate nation, with himself as the chief executive, with New Orleans as the capital. He also planned a military campaign against the Spanish to add Florida and Mexico to his new country. Jefferson had a secret agent named John Graham follow Burr in his various dealings up and down the Mississippi River, and it seemed to Graham that the further Burr traveled, the more support he got for his revolutionary takeover of the West. Jefferson finally decided to have Burr arrested for *"high-treason."* He was tried in a Mississippi court by a three-judge panel and found innocent of the charge. President Jefferson felt the court was rigged and had Burr arrested again by federal troops and brought to federal court on the same charges. Judge John Marshall ruled that *"treason and levying war can only be established by an overt act, and by an assemblage of men in preparation for battle,"* which Burr hadn't done; therefore, he was once more acquitted. Although free, Burr was now a defeated man in body and spirit. His wife had died many years before, in 1794, but he had fathered a daughter, also called Theodosia, who had married at 17, Colonel Joseph Alston, who later became Governor of South Carolina. They had a son, named Aaron Burr

Alston. Burr adored both daughter and grandson, but felt obliged to leave all he loved behind to mourn his losses, and sailed off in self-appointed exile to live in England.

Theodosia Burr Alston's world fell apart four years later when her son came down with a fever and expired in her arms on the morning of June 30, 1812. At about that same time, Aaron Burr quickly left England, for a new war between Britain and America had begun on the 17th of June. Fearing reprisals from old enemies, he disguised himself coming into Boston, sold a few valuable books to the President of Harvard College, and sailed on to New York, incognito. Once in Towne, with the help of old friends, he attempted to once again set up a law practice on Nassau Street, but then Theodosia's letter came and he raged in anguish, unable to work for months.

"Dear Father," the letter read. *"A few miserable days past and your late letters would have gladdened my soul; and even now I rejoice at their contents as much as it is possible for me to rejoice at anything. I have lost my boy. My child is gone forever...My head is not now sufficiently collected to say anything further. May heaven, by other blessings, make you some amends for the noble grandson you have lost. . . Love, Theodosia"*

Theodosia and her father, one in South Carolina and the other in New York, barely made it through the late summer and autumn, both suffering their loss with long illnesses of mind, soul and body. By December, however, Theodosia felt obliged to visit her father, whom she hadn't seen in over five years. Although her husband was opposed to a sea journey, especially in winter after her long illness, Theodosia was adamant. She and her father had always been quite close, and in fact, as a girl after her mother died, she ran the household for him and was hostess at his grand New York parties at their home in Albany. It was he who had personally taught her many languages, how to dance and play the harp and how to become a successful lady in society. One would think that Governor Joseph Alston would be pleased and thankful to Aaron Burr for the proper teaching and training of his wife, but it seems that the governor wasn't overly fond of his father-in-law, and may have been jealous of Theodosia's obsessiveness towards him. Reluctantly, the governor hired a former Carolina privateer, PATRIOT, to transport Theodosia, her maid, excessive baggage, and a portrait of herself by noted artist John Vanderlyn to New York. The painting was to be a gift for her father.

The schooner departed Georgetown, South Carolina on December 30, 1812. Only a few days out of Georgetown, the PATRIOT was hailed by a British man-of-war and was boarded by British tars and officers as part of an on-going blockade of the American coast. Theodosia handed the officers a letter from her husband, requesting safe passage through the blockade, *"as a courtesy to the governor and his wife,"* and the ever-gallant British complied. The PATRIOT headed north for Cape Hatteras to be guided around the shoals by a tall, ever-vigilant Cape Hatteras Lighthouse, fondly called by the locals, *"Hamilton's Light,"* for it was the untiring efforts of Alexander Hamilton that required the building of many lighthouses along the Atlantic coast, and especially the one at Cape Hatteras. His report to the Senate in 1794 read: *"I have for a long time entertained an opinion that a lighthouse on some part of Cape Hatteras should be established, and the lighthouse should be first rate."* As a result, a 90-foot tower was erected in 1798, six years before he was killed by Theodosia's father. Now, eight years after Hamilton's death, one wonders, could Theodosia see the irony of it all? It was her father's enemy's light that was guiding her through treacherous shoal waters. But, possibly, this was Hamilton's sweet revenge. Once rounding Cape Hatteras, the PATRIOT and all crew and passengers, including Theodosia, disappeared and were never heard from again.

When weeks passed and neither Colonel Burr in New York, nor Governor Alston in South Carolina heard a word on the whereabouts of the schooner PATRIOT and their beloved Theodosia, they both sank into deep depression. Alston wrote to Burr on February 11, 1813:

"Authentic accounts from various quarters has already forced upon me the dreadful conviction that we have no more hope... First my boy, now my wife gone, both! This, then, is the end of all the hope we had formed... She was the last tie that bound us to the human race. What have we left?? ... You are the only person in the world with whom I can commune on this subject; for you are, the only person whose feelings can have any community with mine. You know those we loved. Here, none know them; none valued them as they deserved... But the man who has been deemed worthy of the heart of Theodosia Burr, an who has felt what it was to be blessed with such a woman, will never forget her elevation."

Governor Joseph Alston died within three years of Theodosia's disappearance, of what his family concluded was a broken heart. Aaron Burr, lonely and bereft, constantly attempted to find out what happened to his beloved daughter for over 25 years, until his death in 1836. His only clue was that bits of wreckage, thought to have come from the schooner PATRIOT, washed ashore, near Nag's Head, North Carolina, only a few miles from *"Hamilton Light."* Certainly old Colonel Burr saw the tragic irony in his beloved's demise at the foot of his great enemy's monument of light. If Colonel Burr had only humbled himself to inquire at the sprinkling of wreckers' huts along the Nag's Head Beach, he might have discovered a heart-rending revelation – his daughter was not dead, but living in one of those huts.

It wasn't until some fifty years after Aaron Burr had passed away that some light was shed on the fate of the PATRIOT and her beautiful, prestigious passenger. Doctor William Poole of Elizabeth City often visited the fisherfolk who lived in the shacks along the Cape Hatteras beaches, an act of humane charity. They couldn't afford his services, so he offered it free, sometimes accepting a basket of fish in payment for medicine. One of his patients was Lovie Tillet Wescott, almost six feet tall and weighing over 250 pounds. She was in her seventies and took sick for the first time in her life. Doctor Poole treated her, and while in her shack, made up of reed thatch and timbers from old shipwrecks that had washed ashore, he spotted a fine painting of a young woman hanging over Lovie's makeshift mantel. The woman in the portrait was beautiful and welldressed in a low cut gown. Was it her as a young woman, the Doctor asked Lovie, which set her to laughing so hard her body shook. It was not herself, she assured the doctor, but a painting of a woman, taken from a ship wrecked off the beach, and the woman herself was taken from the wreck, *"a poor demented soul, who would hardly let the painting out of her sight."* The painting, Lovie informed the doctor, was given to her, with a trunk of fine gowns, which she still possessed, and a bowl of wax flowers, by a fisherman suitor named Willie Mann, some fifty years earlier. Willie wanted to marry Lovie, and thought the gifts taken from the wreck would help her decide on him as a husband. Lovie accepted the gifts, but instead married fisherman John Wescott. Willie wasn't happy, but he never asked for the gifts back. Lovie said that the gowns never fit her, and she wasn't overly fond of the painting, therefore, if the doctor would accept it for payment for his visit and the medicine that was making her well, she'd gladly give up the painting in payment. Doctor Poole was well aware of the history of wrecking and piracy by the occupants of these shack-dwellings at Nag's Head, and he concluded that Lovie wasn't telling him all that she knew, but he accepted the painting as payment and took it back with him to Elizabeth City, North Carolina.

Friends and neighbors of the good doctor's recognized the painting as a Vanderlyn, noted artist of the early 1800s. Further investigation identified the woman in the portrait, by her black eyes and firm jaw, as Theodosia Burr. John Vanderlyn had also done an oil painting of Aaron Burr in 1802, and thus, Theodosia's surprise for her father was that she had also sat for Vanderlyn in South Carolina, and the portrait was to be his. When the painting miraculously reappeared in the 1880s, members of the Burr family in New York and New Jersey were notified, and eight cousins traveled to Doctor Poole's house in North Carolina to view it. All agreed that it was Theodosia. The painting eventually made its way to its original destination, New York City, where it hangs today in the Macbeth Art Gallery.

Slowly but surely, the truth of what actually happened to Theodosia herself on that fatal voyage became known, through deathbed confessions of three Nag's Head wreckers, dying at different times in different U.S. cities, one being Frank Burdick in Cass County, Michigan, at almost the turn of the century, who admitted under oath that he had assisted in murdering all aboard the PATRIOT. Piecing all three confessions together, which differed on a few minor details, it became apparent that Nag's Head wreckers had displayed a false light some thirty miles down the beach from *"Hamilton Light,"* on that Christmas week of 1812. It was a stormy night, and as planned, the false light on the beach was mistaken by the PATRIOT skipper, Captain Overstocks, of being a lighthouse or another ship. Sailing in, he was caught in the breakers, and both masts snapped off, leaving the schooner helpless. She was soon pounced upon by the piratical wreckers, who boarded her from dories, and although the PATRIOT crew fought them, they were no match in strength of numbers to the wreckers. The few crew members and captain who finally surrendered were shot and thrown overboard with weights around their ankles so they wouldn't ever float to the surface to be identified. The ship was looted of all its treasures, including nautical instruments, fittings, cargo, and Theodosia's belongings. The wreckers, shouting and screaming, and their clothes and weapons covered with innocent blood, discovered Theodosia cowering in her cabin. Her maid, who had actually fought to protect her mistress, was heaved overboard to be devoured by sharks. It was too much for Theodosia who only recently had held the limp form of her dead son in her arms. She went insane right before the wreckers' eyes. She hugged her portrait and cried, *"It's mine, it's mine!"* over and over again. The leader of these butchers, one Dom Dominique, wanted to kill Theodosia right then and there, so there would be no witnesses to their evil deed, but Willie Mann for one, vehemently opposed killing anyone who had gone insane. It was a seaman's taboo to ever harm anyone *"touched in the head."* Willie and a few of the others agreed to have their women care for Theodosia. She was placed in one of the dories with her painting and rowed ashore, and she lived with these wrecker-fishermen in their shacks for many years, often roving the long Nag's Head beach singing to herself or mumbling to the wind. One day she just walked into the thundering surf and never returned to the beach. The wreckers had kept silent of this, as they did of their many misdeeds over the years, until three of them in deathbed confessions revealed the truth. Aaron Burr could have known of his daughter's fate, but maybe it was best he didn't. Not knowing, however, he must have somehow felt Hamilton's hand in the mystery. Here was a great man, who, but for one vote, would have been President of the United States, and because of that vote, lost everything he desired and loved in life – his was a fate worse than death.

Chapter 4
Terror At Minot's Ledge

Just off the coast of Cohasset, Massachusetts, on the southern approach to Boston Harbor by sea, is a series of barely submerged shoals called *"Cohasset Rocks."* The most easterly of these *"rocks"* is Minot's Ledge, some 18 miles from Boston, but only three miles from the great expanse of Nantasket Beach. Only 25 feet long, the ledge is submerged at high tide and barely visible at low tide, but is first to take the brunt and fury of every easterly gale, producing breakers recorded at well over 100 feet. For over two centuries since the first settlement at Boston, Minot's Ledge was not marked as a menace to navigation and therefore was the cause of many a tragic shipwreck. One of the first victims was a sloop owned by Boston merchant Anthony Collamore, which struck the ledge on December 16, 1693, sinking the sloop and drowning Collamore and five others. In 1754, Dorchester merchant George Minot lost his vessel with expensive cargo and all hands lost, thus the name given to the treacherous ledge. The great Danish ship GERTRUDE-MARIA hit there in 1793, and there was another major shipwreck at Minot's on December 6, 1818, when the heavily laden bark SARAH & SUSAN split in two after hitting the ledge, tossing her thirteen-man crew into the raging sea. Four drowned, but the others clung to wreckage and were rescued by Cohasset lifesavers. From 1832 to 1841, there were 42 ships wrecked at Cohasset Rocks, most of them after striking Minot's Ledge. A stone lighthouse was built at Cedar Point in nearby Scituate in 1811 but in 1843, national lighthouse inspector I. P. Lewis condemned it as being *"in partial ruin and threatened with demolition by the sea."*

Inspector Lewis further reported to Congress that *"Ships entering (Boston) with a northeast gale, if they fail of hitting the light-house channel by drifting to the southward, are often wrecked on the lee shore of Cohasset, where a dangerous reef extends about two miles to the northward, and is annually the scene of the most heart-rending disasters, causing the death of many a brave seaman and the loss of large amounts of property... One of the causes of frequent shipwrecks on those rocks has been the lighthouse at Scituate, four miles to leeward of the reef which has been repeatedly mistaken for Boston Light... Not a winter passes without one or more of these fearful accidents occurring... The loss of lives and property will continue to occur until a light is established on this ledge and the one at Scituate suppressed."*

Lewis' suggestion was accepted, and Captain William Swift, of the U.S. Topographical Engineers, was sent to Minot's Ledge to study the feasibility of placing a lighthouse there. Construction would be most difficult, but Swift thought a lighthouse could be built on the ledge. Work could be accomplished only at low tides when the water was calm during the summer months. On good days, the top of the ledge was dry for only two to three hours a day. The work didn't start until 1847, when 21 men began hauling in drilling machinery and supplies, via schooner, to the ledge. The schooner, anchored just off the ledge, was also used as sleeping and eating quarters when the men weren't fighting the elements on the ledge. Twice, drilling machinery and other equipment was swept off the ledge by breakers, and although the men worked with lifelines, they too were often swept from the ledge by rogue waves, but nobody was killed or seriously injured. Because of cold and rough seas, work ceased from late October until mid-May. William Swift had decided to build an iron skeleton structure on the ledge, rather than a stone structure. It could be built faster, and Swift believed that nine iron piles, tapering slightly toward the top, set into holes drilled five feet into the ledge, would be stronger than a stone base. *"The iron piles,"* Swift concluded, *"offer less resistance to the breakers which pass through the uprights than a stone tower against which the waves break with full power."* Above the spidery high legs, the keepers' quarters, lantern room, and a storage room was built. Then, expensive French lanterns with fifteen reflectors, which intensified the rays of the oil lamps, were installed in the tower. They were lighted for the first time on January 1st, 1850, celebrated with bonfires on the mainland.

During the three years that the lighthouse was being built, however, there were three major shipwrecks at Minot's Ledge. In November of '47, the ship ALABAMA struck Minot's Ledge, then drifted and sank into deep water. She carried a shipment of women's wear, and much was later salvaged to be sold at dirt-cheap prices to the ladies of Boston and Cohasset. The JENNY LIND hit the ledge some twelve months later and wrecked on Scituate Beach. The worst disaster was that of the SAINT JOHN out of Galway, Ireland, filled with Irish immigrants heading for Boston and a new life in America. The SAINT JOHN was one of the infamous "coffin-ships, " an old rotting hulk that should have been chopped up for fireplace wood many years earlier, but was kept afloat to transport the poor, starving Irish of the potato famine. In the midst of a three-day October 1849 storm, Captain Oliver of the SAINT JOHN attempted to anchor his leaking ship off Minot's Ledge, in sight of the unlit, unmanned lighthouse. The old ship dragged her anchors and slid inside the ledge, ripping out her bottom on the rocks. Mainlanders watched her break up before their eyes, but could do nothing, for the waves were too treacherous to attempt rescue. Those who didn't go down with the ship, drowned trying to swim for shore – only Captain Oliver and eleven others in a lifeboat made it to the mainland and safety. Of the 143 people aboard the SAINT JOHN who lost their lives, one was Patrick Swaney. He watched eleven of his children drown, and then he, too, was taken by the sea. On the day after the disaster, Henry David Thoreau visited the wreck site from Concord. *"I was surprised,"* said he, *"at the power of the waves, and that an iron vessel would be cracked up like an egg-shell on the rocks. Some of her timbers, however,"* he went on to say, *"were so rotten that I could almost thrust my umbrella through them."*

There were many letters to the Boston newspapers predicting that the new spindlelegged structure standing some 85 feet above Minot's Ledge would not withstand severe storms. Builder and designer Captain Swift considered their fears ridiculous. The first keeper of Minot's Light, Isaac Dunham, however, refuted the designer's confidence in the structure. Only a few weeks as keeper on the new structure, Dunham wrote this into the log:

"February 5, 1850 – This day and last night will long be remembered by me as one of the most trying that I ever experienced during my life. The wind is NorEast to East, blowing very hard with a sea running mountains high."

"Feb 6 – The wind East, blowing hard with an ugly sea which makes the lighthouse reel like a drunken man. I hope God in His mercy will still this raging sea, or we must perish. God only knows what the end will be. At 4 p.m. the gale continues with great fury. It appears to me that if the wind continues from the East as it is now, we cannot survive the night..."

"Feb 8 – The wind now West by Northwest, blowing very fresh, which will kill the ground sea. Thanks be to God for this blessed wind."

Keeper Dunham wrote to the government asking that the lighthouse be somehow strengthened on its perilous perch, but Captain Swift, displeased at Dunham's letter, assured the government that his lighthouse would hold in any weather. Isaac Dunham resigned as keeper in October of 1850, refusing to spend another winter at Minot's Ledge.

Captain Swift quickly found a more daring lighthouse keeper in an old British Navy salt named Captain John Bennett. Bennett publicly made fun of his predecessor Isaac Dunham, calling him everything but a coward, and even worse, a *"landlubber."* Like the keeper before him, Bennett was allowed two assistants, and he chose another Englishman, 20 year old Joe Wilson, and a young Portuguese sailor named Joe Antoine. Bennett and the two Joes weren't at the light a full month when they experienced a wild Nor'easter that lasted for three days, and set the lighthouse to quivering. After the storm, keeper Bennett wrote to the National Superintendent of Lighthouses, Philip Greeley, stating that he thought the lighthouse was in danger of capsizing. Greely formed a government committee that went to Minot's Ledge to investigate. They concluded that *"Minot's Light is capable of weathering any storm without danger."*

On the morning of Friday, April 11, 1851, Keeper Bennet flew a signal flag from the lighthouse, asking for a boat to pick him up so that he might visit the mainland. The lighthouse dory had been smashed in a previous storm and Bennett wanted to go to the Boston Custom House to procure another. He left the two Joes in charge of the lighthouse. When Bennett tried to return to Minot's Light the next day, a storm kicked up, and the seas were too rough to land at the ledge. The storm soon became a gale, and by April 16th, it was a roaring hurricane with winds over 100 miles an hour from the east causing the lighthouse to sway dangerously. Over 100-foot waves continuously smashed into and over the structure, pounding it relentlessly until two of its spidery legs let go and the lighthouse tilted to a twenty-degree angle. The two young lighthouse assistants were petrified. They kept the light going until about 10 p.m. – that's the last anyone on the mainland saw it. Three hours later, the lighthouse fogbell could be heard on the mainland over the screams of the wind and pounding of the surf. In the pitch blackness, it was being rung manually by the two Joes, obviously as a cry for help, but there was no one that could help them – it was their death knell. When the sound of the bell stopped, the lighthouse toppled into the sea.

At daylight, when a boat was able to make it to Minot's Ledge, there were only a few bent piles protruding some four to six feet from the rock. There was no lighthouse and no keepers. A day later, a Gloucester fisherman picked up a bottle floating on the surface near Hingham Harbor. In it was a note from the two Joes. It read: *"Wednesday night, April 16 – The lighthouse won't stand over tonight. She shakes two feet each way now – J. W.: and J.A."* The bottle and note are now the property of the Hingham Historical Society.

Joseph Antoine's body washed ashore on Nantasket Beach. Joe Wilson was found at Gull Rock, his body bruised and cut. He had crawled to the top of the rock, probably thinking that he had made the mainland shore, only to discover that he was on a tiny island, still far from shore. He died of exposure and not from drowning. Captain William Smith was devastated; his unshakable lighthouse had toppled, as many had predicted. Minot's Ledge was once again without light and once again beckoned ships and sailors to their doom.

An old Delaware Bay lightship was towed to Minot's Ledge to keep a light burning off this most treacherous shoal, and the old lighthouse keeper, Bennett, was placed in charge of her. After being moored off the ledge only three months, a government inspection team boarded her and found her *"unfit for the job of replacing Minot's Light."* In part, the report of the inspection team read that, *"this boat ought not to be kept in so important a place, and it will be impossible to keep her at her moorings during the winter months."* It was decided to build a new, sturdier lightship for this hazardous duty, and about the same time, plans were presented by the Corps of Engineers to build a new lighthouse at the ledge. This time, however, it was decided that a tower of stone would be more seaworthy than Swift's iron spider-legs design.

The engineer in charge of construction, Barton Alexander, attempted to land on the ledge on May 1st, 1855, to begin work, but the sea wouldn't allow him. He had to wait eleven days to begin removing the old twisted iron from the stone sockets and begin laying great granite slabs, which were fitted to each other and then cemented to the ledge. In the first year, the stone foundation was laid and the iron framework of the structure was installed and painted red before Alexander and his men were forced to leave the ledge for the winter. When he returned the following spring, he discovered the structure had disappeared – all their previous year's work had been in vain. Alexander felt that if nature had such fury to collapse what he considered an indestructible structure, then to build a lighthouse at Minot's Ledge was folly. He remained dejected for only a few days, however, for he then was told that the bark NEW EMPIRE had struck Minot's Ledge in a January storm, with such impact that she had demolished the newly erected structure. When the greatly damaged ship was inspected, great globs of red paint were discovered on her bent and twisted side, meaning that a sturdy ship and not the ocean had demolished Alexander's work, which, ironically, gave the builder new hope – he might, he thought, yet conquer the elements at Minot's Ledge.

The final stone to the new 114-foot-tall Minot's Light was laid on June 29, 1860, exactly five years from the day Alexander and his workman began the structure, and 9 1/2 years since Swift's tower collapsed. The new keeper was Joshua Wilder and his two assistants were A. Williams and William Taylor, extremely brave souls, considering what had happened to their predecessors. The new lamp was lit on November 15, 1860, at dusk, and as with the old light, there were great celebrations on the mainland when the lamp was lit – bonfires, fireworks, and the tooting of horns and whistles from shore – the most treacherously located lighthouse in America was, once more, up and running. Debate was then, as it was back in 1850, will she withstand the heavy seas and powerful breakers of a New England Nor'easter? Today, some 150 years later, we can answer with a resounding "Yes," for Alexander's light, although noticeably trembling through many a wild storm, has survived to this day.

The real terror in the new lighthouse, it seems, is not the fierce storms, but a strange unexplained phenomenon. Fishermen, who often pass close by the lighthouse at night, report hearing cries, moans and pleadings for help from the base of the structure. A Portuguese crew swore to the keeper that they saw a man in the moonlight, hanging from the lighthouse outer ladder, as waves were breaking over him. He held onto the rungs for dear life. Sailing in to help the man, he shouted to them in their native tongue, *"Stay away, stay away!"* but then he vanished. From that day to this, Portuguese fishermen usually avoid sailing near Minot's Ledge, believing that the spirit of their countryman, possibly the ghost of assistant keeper Joe Antoine, appears to warn them away. The spirits of the two Joes of the original lighthouse have also been felt inside the new lighthouse, and supposedly prompted the first keeper, Joshua Wilder, to leave his post less than a year after accepting it. Shadowy figures seen in the lensroom, taps on the shoulders from unseen hands during night watches, whispering voices filling the night air in the tower – it was just too much for the sensitive Josh Wilder.

One night, a few years later, Keeper Per Tornberg, a no-nonsense Swede who didn't believe in ghosts, was in the lighthouse watchroom when he tapped his pipe on the table ashtray to knock out the old ashes. To his surprise, he heard a loud similar tapping from below in response. He tapped his pipe again five times, and received five similar taps from the bowels of the structure. The assistant keeper was asleep in an adjoining alcove, so Tornberg knew the tapping was not being repeated by a human. What further distressed him was the fact that the five-tap code was the signal in the old lighthouse that one shift was over, and that the assistant, Joe Antoine or Joe Wilson, should climb to the lensroom to begin a new shift. Many keepers from that night on have tapped out the code and received the five-tap response, some believing it to be the spirits of the two Joes, others concluding it is just the coincidental creaking of the stone structure. There have been other incidents, however, over the years, that have persuaded keepers and their assistants that the two Joes from the old spider-legged light haunt Minot's Ledge. One periodic happening that chills the lighthouse occupants is the cleaning of the lenses by unseen hands. The lighthouse lenses must be squeaky clean at all times, for dirt or dust will dull and deflect the light; plus, quantities of seabird droppings on the outer glass can dim the power of the light considerably. Keepers at Minot's have found the glass already cleaned, when only seconds before, they had instructed an assistant to polish it because the lens or glass was dirty – a job that often takes hours. Herbert Reamy, who became keeper in 1887, repeatedly found dirty glass cleaned in an instant if he mentioned it to an assistant, and he had no doubt it was the spirit of the Joes who accomplished this task in seconds, whereas it might take all day for a live assistant to do it. Reamy often thanked the two Joes audibly for their neatness and lighthouse discipline. He said it helped keep him sane. One keeper, after Reamy's vigil, slit his throat with a razor and bled to death inside the lighthouse before his body was discovered by an assistant, and another Minot's Light keeper went insane and was shipped off the ledge in a straight-jacket – both, so others assumed, were either victims of the gloomy grey winter seas, or the hauntings of the two Joes. Even a lighthouse cat, brought to the ledge for companionship by a keeper, went berserk when it arrived in the tower, chasing around in circles as if possessed, and when the keeper opened a door to an outside upper deck platform, the cat leaped off the platform and fell some fifty feet, dashing itself upon the ledge and being swept away by a breaker. Maybe the spirits drove it berserk.

Obviously, the wild seas of Minot's Light, or the tidy pranks of ghosts there, will unnerve the most courageous of man or beast, but today, Minot's Light is vacant of life.

Only the two Joes, with the help of automation, keep the light glowing each night, with a beam shining some fifteen miles out to sea, directing ships to the entrance of Boston Harbor, and away from the hazardous Cohasset Rocks.

Woodcut of spindle-legged Minot's Light off Cohasset, Massachusetts, tumbles from its perch in an April 1851 storm, killing two assistant keepers.

Rebuilding Minot's Light on the infamous ledge in 1859.
U.S. Coast Guard photo.

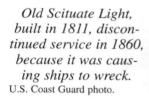

Old Scituate Light, built in 1811, discontinued service in 1860, because it was causing ships to wreck.
U.S. Coast Guard photo.

Minot's Light today.
U.S. Coast Guard photo.

Teenagers Abigail and Rebecca Bates, daughters of the Scituate Lighthouse Keeper, played military music on fife and drum to frighten off British marines in September, 1814. Their bluff saved the town and the lighthouse.
1864 sketch from St. Nicholas Magazine.

Boston Lighthouse at the mouth of Boston Harbor, America's first lighthouse, erected in 1717. It was nearly destroyed completely by the British and the Americans during the Revolutionary War. The tower pictured here, built in 1783, still stands, and is the last to be manned by Coast Guardsmen.
Photo courtesy Early Sites Research

Highland Light, better known as Cape Cod Light, built in 1797.

Lovell Island range-lights, built in 1902. Keeper Charles Jennings found old coins of silver and gold in the garden behind the keeper's house, thought to come from the wreck of the French warship MAGNIFIQUE.

Chapter 5
The Boston Beacons

Since the 1620's, a lone mariner named Blackstone, lived with the Shawmut Indians atop Beacon Hill, where the Massachusetts State House now stands. Besides building a home for himself on the hill, and planting an apple orchard, the hermit Blackstone also provided a constant nightly fire to guide trading vessels into Boston harbor for exchange of goods for himself and the Indians. In 1630, Governor Winthrop arrived with English settlers across the river at what is now Charlestown, and because of the lack of good drinking water there, moved across the river with his group of Puritans to Boston. Blackstone soon felt crowded and moved out to the wilds of what is now Rhode Island, but the Puritans continued his ritual of keeping a fire burning atop Beacon Hill as a guide for incoming ships. Although Blackstone's beacon continued to be an aide to mariners and fishermen for many years, the wind and wave-swept reefs and islands of Boston harbor destroyed a high percentage of ships and valuable cargoes.

The inner harbor has many deep anchorages, but *"there are many small islands before Boston,"* wrote visitor Peter Sluyter in 1680, *"well unto fifty, I believe, between which you sail on to the town."* One sea captain called the Boston harbor islands and reefs, *"tombstones of shattered ships,"* commenting that getting into Boston docks and piers was like *"threading a needle."* Boston author Robert Sullivan describes the traditional harbor channel coming into Boston as *"a confined tunnel, especially on a pitch black night amid raging winds, beset by bone-chilling cold and surging sea. Add to this nerve-wracking passage a bit of compass deviation, drift impelled by insidious tidal currents, and perhaps a slight miscalculation in plotting."* Such condition often makes the attempt to get into the harbor *"a fatal end to a long voyage on the very threshold of home port."* Add to the above, the deep religious belief of the Puritans that the Devil himself lived amongst them and was ever-ready to deploy demons and witch-imps into their midst, and the life of a Boston mariner was indeed fearful and perilous, especially in the seventeenth century.

Prior to the Puritan witch hysteria of 1692 at Salem, some 13 miles from Boston, where twenty were executed for witchcraft, Boston hanged a few witches of her own in the 1640s. One was Margaret Jones, her crime was providing remedies for sick neighbors. Margaret's husband, with good reason, decided to leave Boston Town after his wife was executed, and he boarded the ship WELCOME in the Autumn of 1648, bound for England. The ship's log records that in Boston harbor, *"the weather was calm, yet the ship fell to rolling, and so deep it was feared she would flounder. A great weight was placed on one side to trim her, and she would heel over to the other side."* Passing the islands on the way out to sea, the captain found it impossible to control his ship, and fearing he would wreck on one of the many harbor islands, he tactfully turned the WELCOME around and returned to port. There seemed no logical reason for the vessel to be acting so strangely except for one; at the dockside, the captain was told that the husband of an executed witch was aboard. The County Court happened to be in session at Boston, and the captain of the WELCOME had the sheriff arrest Thomas Jones and place him in jail. Like his wife, he was accused of witchcraft. No sooner was Thomas behind bars that *"the ship ceased to rolling, and it moved no more."* The WELCOME left Boston and arrived safely in England, all aboard thankful that they had discovered the Devil's witch aboard before leaving on their voyage.

Even though a makeshift wood burning beacon was placed at Point Allerton, a long peninsula jutting into the mouth of Boston harbor, in 1673, vessels continued to wreck or founder in fogs and storms at Harding's Ledge, Graves Ledge, Shag Rock and Devil's Back, all located near or in the harbor entrance. In 1678, a courageous soul named Captain James Oliver was sent by the Boston Puritan fathers to live at the desolate Point Allerton to tend the island beacon full time, yet, major disasters continued to plague Boston Harbor. Into the early eighteenth century, valuable cargoes of wine, rum, salt and log-wood were lost, as were many lives from the ships MARY, JOHN OF EXON, PROVIDENCE, and the King's schooner, HAZARD. Boston was fast becoming America's most important and active port, yet mariners were reluctant to enter the harbor because of its many hazards and lack of navigational aides, especially at night. It wasn't until July of 1715 that the magistrates finally took action. A court bill read that, *"Whereas the want of a lighthouse at the entrance to the harbour of Boston hath been a great discouragement to navigation by the loss of the lives and estates of several of his majesty's subjects; for preservation thereof, Be it enacted that there be a lighthouse erected at the charge of the Province, on the southmost part of the Great-Brewster Island, to be kept lighted from the sun setting to sun rising."* Thus commenced the building of America's first lighthouse.

The stone tower lighthouse was completed in two years, but on Little Brewster, not Great Brewster Island, as directed in the official order, the smaller island facing the sea providing easier access to vessels approaching the narrow channel at the mouth of the harbor. The keeper was also provided a fog bell to be rung manually and a cannon to warn off vessels from the reef on foggy or stormy nights, and as a defense against pirates or enemies. If such unwanted guests approached the harbor, the keeper was to fly the Union Jack from the lighthouse, warning the mainlanders and spattering of inner islanders that an enemy or pirate band was about to enter Boston waters, giving the population plenty of time to prepare a defense. The keeper was also to act as a pilot, personally meeting every cargo ship and guiding her into the inner harbor, for a fee. It was a lucrative job, but there were few mainlanders who were willing to live on a lonely storm-swept spit of land facing the open sea, twelve miles from town. Finally, an old man who had grown up on the outer islands, volunteered to be America's first lighthouse keeper. He was George Worthylake, who moved into the lighthouse with his wife and two daughters on September 14, 1716. The coal-burning lamp was lit. To add to his income, Worthylake brought with him some sixty sheep to fatten on the island saltgrasses. But one of his first of many complaints of life on Little Brester, now called "Beacon Island," was that many of his flock drowned while feeding on grasses at low tide, only to be swept out to sea when the tide came in.

Worthylake and his family endured for almost twenty-six months, but on November 3, 1718, a tragedy occurred which prompted the superstitious mariners and mainlanders to spread the rumor that Boston Light was cursed. On that morning of calm seas, the keeper, with his wife, daughter Ruth, and their black slave named Shadwell, had gone into town so that Worthylake could collect his pay. He had left his older daughter Ann with a girlfriend to tend the light in their absence. On the way back to the lighthouse, Worthylake picked up a passenger named John Edge at Lovell Island and then proceeded in their double-ended boat to Little Brewster. As the five approached the lighthouse in their seemingly seaworthy craft, it, for some unknown reason, capsized. All aboard were drowned, with Ann and her friend looking on helplessly from the lighthouse. *"We saw them overset in their boat,"* Ann later reported, *"at about noon that day, all swimming or floating in the water in distress, but I can say nothing further."* When the body of the keeper was recovered, the pay he had collected from Boston was not in his pocket and some suspicious mainlanders thought there might have been foul play. Ann, the only surviving daughter of keeper Worthylake, thought not. Rumors persisted however, that members of the Waters family who lived on Lovell Island and had recovered the bodies, took the money from the dead keeper's pocket.

The mysterious drownings and the possibility of corpse robbing, so excited Bostonians, that a poem about the tragedy was written by a 13 year old boy and printed for distribution around town by the boy's brother. In part, it read: *"Quick the prow is upward borne George in Ann's arms tossed, Husband, wife and child together, In the chilly waves are lost."* Later in life, the acclaimed poet said his *"Lighthouse Tragedy"* was *"wretched stuff"* – the poet was Benjamin Franklin.

The lighthouse was now without a keeper and nobody wanted the job. The court, in special session, ordered a sea captain named Robert Saunders to *"Go to Beacon Island and take care of the lighthouse."* Within a week of the order, Captain Robert Saunders was found floating in Boston harbor, drowned under mysterious circumstances. There is no doubt now in the minds of the Puritanical Bostonians that the lighthouse was cursed. Yet, town fathers prevailed on *"an experienced mariner and discreet person,"* named John Hayes to attend the lighthouse. Hayes, it seems, was plagued by new demons, not experienced by the previous keeper – the most prevalent being the demon rum. Hayes decided that to make a little extra money, he would sell liquor and provide other treats for the captains of incoming ships. Apparently these indulgences got out of hand, for he wrote to the town fathers shortly after taking his position that *"I have given off entertainment, finding the same prejudicial to myself as well as the Town of Boston."* Hayes also had trouble with a group of local merchant sailors known as the "boardinghouse runners," who would camp at the Brewsters each day in the summer, and sail out in small boats to meet incoming ships, attempting to sell foreign sailors rum and various other treats, including women. Some also disguised themselves as pilots and collected fees for escorting foreign vessels into the inner harbor, which, of course, reduced the number of fees keeper Hayes could collect. He complained bitterly to the authorities, and although some attempts were made to stop the runners, their enterprise was too vast and constantly moving to other islands to completely control. Three other demons reared their ugly heads at the lighthouse in the early years of the eighteenth century – fire, ice and plague. A fire almost consumed the light and keeper Hayes on January 13, 1720. Hayes said that *"the lamps dropping on ye wooden benches and snuff falling off, it set a fire,"* driving him out of the light-tower and causing over 200-pounds sterling in damages until he was able to snuff it out. Summoned to a board of inquiry at Boston, Hayes swore that *"ye said fire was not occasioned by the least bit of neglect,"* yet his pay was withheld until the repairs were made and the lighthouse was in service again. There was also rumor in town that Hayes, in his solitary confinement at the light, had taken to consuming rum which he took in payment for piloting ships.

Ice sometimes stranded and wrecked more vessels in the harbor than fog and rough wind, and Hayes complained that *"Ice and snow greatly obscure the glass of the lighthouse."* The ice in the harbor also prevented Hayes from getting into town for supplies. Two great storms of 1723 and 1727, did great damage to the lighthouse and both times tore away the lighthouse pier, further stranding the nervous keeper. He complained that the lighthouse shook violently during these storms. To further aggravate the keeper, many ships from the British Isles began arriving with immigrants, mostly from Ireland and Scotland in the 1730s, some diseased and others that were dead or dying. Hayes was the designated health inspector, adding twenty pounds to his annual salary, but his fear of contracting the deadly plague himself, forced him into a self-imposed retirement in 1733.

During the early stages of the American Revolution, the British blocked the entrance to Boston Harbor and took over operation of the lighthouse, but on July 20, 1775, a band of Colonial troops rowed out to the Brewsters and set the lighthouse on fire. Rowing home, after only slight resistance from the British, a

Colonial soldier commented that, *"the flames of the lighthouse ascended up to heaven like grateful incense."* Only the wooden portion of the lighthouse destroyed, the British began to repair it, with a large contingent of British marines guarding the workmen on the island. This time it was Commander George Washington himself, headquartered in nearby Cambridge, who gave the order to destroy the lighthouse, and he sent Major Ben Tupper and 300 men in whaleboats on a midnight row to the island from Dorchester. The "Battle of Boston Light" was won by the Colonials and the lighthouse was once more destroyed by fire, but upon retreating back to the mainland, the whaleboats were attacked by British ships. The Americans, however, lost only one man and the British suffered heavy casualties. By the time the British were forced to evacuate Boston, on March 17, 1776, they had rebuilt the lighthouse once again, but their last vessel out of the harbor, deposited a team of Redcoats on Little Brewster and they blew up the lighthouse. It was not, however, completely destroyed, and was rebuilt by the Colonials in 1783. Never in the history of lighthouses or war has a beacon been destroyed and rebuilt so many times within such a short period. It seems that Boston Light was still living up to its reputation of being cursed, but like the nation itself, when knocked down, she always managed to return to her duty.

Seven years later, the United States Government took over the running of Boston Light, and Thomas Knox became the new keeper, where he remained until 1811. That same year, another new lighthouse was built at nearby Scituate, but shipwrecks continued in this area, mainly because sea captains now confused Scituate Light with Boston Light. The appointed keeper at Cedar Point, Scituate, was Simeon Bates, and with him he brought a son and two young daughters. The daughters, Abigail and Rebecca were soon to become national heroes, for on September 7, 1814, the great British man-o-war LA-HOGUE anchored off Scituate Harbor and sent five longboats filled with marines in towards the lighthouse. The War of 1812 was on, and the British were bent on revenge for defeats in the Revolution. Keeper Bates was in town at the time and the two teenaged girls, seeing the invasion party on its way in, sent their younger brother scurrying to town to warn the citizens. Bold Rebecca, however, had an idea to delay the Redcoats. She played the flute, and there was an old Revolutionary drum in the attic of the keeper's house. Abigail fetched it. They ran for the cover of a nearby sand-dune, close to the channel where British boats must pass to get to the lighthouse, and they began playing and drumming as loud as they could, marching up and down behind the dune as the music blared out over the ocean. It was the same music the Colonial drummers and fifers played to rally the troops before battle, and the sound of it was enough to make the boats filled with marines retreat back to their mother ship. The LA HOGUE soon lifted anchor and was on her way to attack some other defenseless port. The town folks who had witnessed the retreat, saw the

LA HOGUE send one cannon ball screaming at the lighthouse before she sailed off, but it missed the tower by some forty yards. The Bates girls were cheered and congratulated for fending off what could have been a devastating attack by the British, and the national lighthouse service awarded them medals for bravery. The light itself, however, still remained a hazard to navigation, even though its white light was changed to flashing red. In November 1860, when Minot's Light was finally up and running, the government snuffed out Scituate Light, but the lighthouse remains standing to this day, preserved as a memorial to courageous keepers and the patriotic Bates girls.

It was another American hero, John Paul Jones, who, in August 1782, was in Boston awaiting the arrival of the great 74-gun French man-o-war MAG-NIFIQUE, a gift to America from the French king, but Paul was seriously disappointed. The assistant keeper of the Boston Light, David Darling, while piloting the French vessel through the narrow channel off Lovell Island, inside the harbor, wrecked the gift on Ram's Head Flats, now called *"Man-O-War Bar."* Down with the ship went a cargo of gold and silver coins, also a gift to the struggling new country from France. No lives were lost, but it was an expensive mistake for the keeper-pilot, and was very embarrassing for him and our nation. Over the years, sand and silt covered the wreck forming a new bar, which became an added hazard in the channel. Four years later, on December 4, 1786, a passenger ship carrying fifteen people hit the bar. No one was living on the island, so as the ship broke apart, the passengers had to swim to the island. In the midst of a blizzard, they attempted to find shelter on their own, but there was none. When the storm subsided, all fifteen were discovered in the snow frozen to death. Two, who were lovers, were found high on Lovell Island's hill, frozen together in an embrace. The boulder they had hidden behind for protection against the cold is still called, "Lover's Rock." A refuge hut was built on the island for shipwreck victims the following year and although obviously needed, a lighthouse wasn't erected on Lovell Island until 1902. Then, the government built two of them, both small but effective range lights. To run the lights, Boston Light Keeper, Charles Jennings, was transferred to Lovell Island, and although he didn't like the move, it proved to be quite prosperous for him. While planting a garden behind the keeper's house, he came across fistfuls of blackened discs. Washing them off, he found them to be gold and silver French coins. They were treasure from the MAGNIFIQUE, which had now become part of the island's landmass, just off Man-O-War Bar. Jennings retrieved about $7,000 worth of coins, but he always felt that his assistant, who did some digging in the garden when the keeper was away on the mainland, may have come up with the lion's share, for he soon quit his job and moved West. People were still digging for MAGNIFIQUE treasure on Lovell Island in 1998. The lights were removed from the island during World War II, but the keeper's house and his garden are still there.

One cannot find fault with Keeper Jennings or his assistant for making a fast buck while working in a profession that was never known to be lucrative, and many keepers performed extra duties or worked at other avocations to make extra money or just to make ends meet. Arnold Johnson, Chief Clerk of the U.S. Lighthouse Board in the 1880s, alerted all keepers and their assistants that they were *"forbidden to engage in any business which can interfere with their presence at their stations or with the proper and timely performance of their lighthouse duties. But it is no unusual thing to find a keeper working at his station as a shoe-maker,"* said Johnson, *"or a tailor, or in some other capacity, and there are still lighthouse keepers who fill a neighboring pulpit, who hold commissions of justice of the peace, and there are still others who do duty as school teachers without resigning their lighthouses."*

Joshua Snow, who became keeper of Boston Light in October 1844, was noted for selling fish dinners and clam and fish chowders to passengers and crew of passing vessels. His operation was so successful, that he gave up being a keeper within four years, moved to neighboring Gallop's Island, which he purchased, and built an inn which prospered under his care and where he personally prepared seafood specialties. Canned Snow's Clam Chowder is still a big seller in grocery stores, and is often the base of chowders sold in restaurants throughout America. Tobias Cook, who replaced Snow as keeper, only lasted a year, for it was discovered that he had started an illegal Spanish cigar factory at the lighthouse. He shipped young girls to the island to roll cigars and then brought the cigars into Boston, selling them as genuine Spanish cigars, making himself a fine profit. The scheme was soon discovered, the girls were fired, and Cook was forced to resign as keeper.

The keeper replacing Cook was less industrious than his predecessors. Keeper Bill Long did, however, have a beautiful daughter named Lucy, who made history at the old lighthouse. Fishermen and pilots would stop frequently at the island to spend time with Lucy, but her favorite seemed to be fisherman Albert Small. One day Albert escorted Lucy to the top of the lighthouse, where she was helping her father in his duties to light the lamp, and there, Albert proposed marriage. It was a first for Boston Light, and their marriage in June of 1853 produced many nautical men and women of future generations, including four lighthouse keepers. Joshua Snow's famous lighthouse keeper's daughter, Peggy, experienced a different ending to her love story. Peggy, more than any other, had helped her father succeed in his chowder business, and like Lucy Long, she fell in love with a local fisherman while attending Boston Light. His name was Ephraim Quiner. When Ephraim was out fishing, Peggy would climb to the island's hill to watch for his boat coming in with the day's catch. Instead of bringing his boat to the pier, if the tide was right, the daring Ephraim would ride his boat straight onto the beach of a spit of land on the edge of Gallop's Island. Peggy would rush from the hill to the beach to embrace him. One late afternoon, after an unusually severe wind storm had swept into the Boston area, Peggy waited, but there was no sign of Ephraim's boat. She stood all night and well into the next day, until her father came to bring her home. Peggy returned to the hill and walked the beach near the spit of sand where Ephraim once landed his boat, every night for the rest of her life, but her fisherman never came in. Her vigil was first known only among the fishermen and other mariners, but over the years, all Bostonian's knew the heart-wrenching story of Peggy Snow. Even as an old infirmed woman, at the end of the day, Peggy would have friends bundle her up and take her carriage to the spit of sand at Gallop's Island, so that she might squint out to sea in search of her fisherman. Today, the spit of sand is named in her memory, *"Peggy's Point,"* and it is where she was buried.

Boston Light and those lighthouses in and around Boston which were erected later, for some unknown reason, seem to elicit romantic tragedy. Deer Island Light, for example, only a few miles in from Boston Light, first illuminated in 1898, became the new home for lovers Wesley and Josaphine Pingree, who spent their honeymoon there as first keeper and assistant keeper. A few years later, Assistant Keeper Frank Sibley proposed marriage in the lighthouse to a local Winthrop girl, Florence Lyndon. Like the Smalls of Boston Light, the Sibleys lived happily thereafter. Joe McCabe, keeper at Deer Island in 1916, left his post one Sunday evening to address wedding invitations on the mainland with his fiancée, but while doing so, a storm began brewing and a cold snap set in. McCabe decided he should return to the lighthouse early, but he found his dory at waters edge frozen to the earth, and he couldn't break it loose from the ice, so he attempted to walk the granite bar at Winthrop to his lighthouse. He apparently slipped on the rocks and fell into the ocean, for on his way to his lighthouse duties, he disappeared and his body was never found.

Fatal romance also seems to be mysteriously present at Egg Rock, a small outcropping of granite that looks like a stranded whale, just three miles out from Nahant, Massachusetts, north of Boston and Winthrop. A lighthouse was built there in 1856, but even then it had a sad history. Blooming in a little patch of earth at the top of this rock outcropping, is a garden of wild flowers, predominantly forget-me-nots. Even from the mainland beaches one can see the slim crown of blue atop the boulders. Italian born, Michael Pitro, strolling with his betrothed one fine summer day along the beach, asked her if she would like a bouquet of the wild flowers. The sea seemed a bit choppy, but she said she would, if he could do it quickly. Young and strong, Michael, a local fisherman, jumped into his dory and rowed as fast as he could to the island, climbed the rocks, picked the flowers, and waved to her from his perch atop Egg Rock. He then scurried back down to his boat and began his row back to the beach. A sudden squall took him by surprise. His boat flooded and soon sank. Seeing his boat go down, his bride-to-be screamed for help. Many locals gathered at the beach, but the sea was too rough for others to help. Soon, Michael drifted ashore in the surf. He had drowned, but clenched in his fist was a bunch of freshly picked forget-me-nots.

In the winter, Egg Rock is often iced in, with great sheets of ice many inches thick forming around it and loose bergs surrounding the island, making it impossible to get in or out until the spring thaw. Such was the case when Lighthouse Keeper Matthew Hicks' wife suddenly died in December. She had been diagnosed earlier with a bad heart, so Hicks wasn't overly shocked, but he was deeply saddened. He personally dressed her in her finest clothes, and himself in black, and flew the distress flag from the lighthouse. No one came out to Egg Rock to help him, and there was no way he could get off the island until the ice melted. He soon realized that this might be months, so he carried Margaret in her finest to the oil shed, and laid her there. Within two days she was frozen solid, and there she stayed until late March, well preserved and seemingly content. When the thaw came, Hicks laid her out in the back seat of his boat and rowed her to shore. He carried her to the funeral parlor where the wake was held immediately and the funeral three hours later. Hicks had made it clear to friends and family on the mainland that he had to be back to the lighthouse before evening set in so he could light the lamp. After Margaret was buried, Matthew just had enough time to visit the home of an old childhood sweetheart in Nahant. She was recently widowed and Matthew proposed that she marry him. He did not want to return to his lonely outpost alone. She, at first, refused, but consented two hours later, just before dusk. She quickly packed her bags as Matthew summoned a preacher, and just as the sun was setting, Matthew, with his new bride, was rowing hell-bent for Egg Rock to perform his duties. He had buried one wife and married another, all within a day-such is the life of a lighthouse keeper. Egg Rock Light was automated in 1919, but then shut down for good in 1922. The lighthouse and the keeper's quarters were then auctioned off to a highest bidder, with the agreement that the units would be removed from the island. This was attempted, but in trying to move the lighthouse to a barge, the cables snapped and the lighthouse and keeper's house plunged into the sea, and in pieces, over the years, washed ashore to the mainland.

The most tragic of love stories began on the evening of the worst shipwreck in Boston Harbor history, November 3, 1861. The square-rigged, 990-ton MARITANA, heading into Boston Harbor after sailing peacefully across the Atlantic from Liverpool, England, smashed into Shag Rocks off Boston Light in a snow squall and heavy seas. Besides cargo of wool, coal and iron, there were 38 crew members and passengers aboard her, under command of Captain George Williams. The bow of the ship was caught in the jagged rocks, with great waves crashing over the deck. The crew managed to cut away the masts at the commander's order, but the vessel was soon broken in half by the rocks and there was no chance of saving her. The captain went down with his ship, and seven managed to float over the shoals on the MARITANA's pilothouse. Five others swam for the lighthouse, where Keeper Moses Barrett looked on in horror. These were the only survivors. Twenty-six men and women either drowned, were battered to death by the rocks, or froze to death on the rock out-croppings as the snowstorm raged on. There was no way the keeper of Boston Light could help them, even though they had wrecked right on his doorstep. At dawn, some five hours after the vessel struck, Keeper Barrett sent a distress signal to the Hull Lifesaving Station across the harbor, and the pilot-boat STARKEY braved the storm, with Sam James of the famous James lifesaving family at her wheel. He and his crew saved the seven clinging to the pilot-house. The Boston Herald reported, "*A more complete wreck was never seen. Fragments of the ship and her freight are strewn over all the lower islands, and occasionally, a mangled body is thrown up on the jagged rocks. God save us all from a death like this.*" Wreckage and bodies covered Little Brewster Island, and Shag Rocks kept spewing them up, the last of the crewmembers being washed ashore at the lighthouse four months later. The sailor's body was buried on the island. At about that same time, the wife and children of Captain Williams came to the lighthouse and the keeper gave them the Captain's watch and other keepsakes that had been found and he had been saving for them. They just sat for hours by the lighthouse looking out at the foaming waves at Shag Rocks that had taken husband and father. Keeper Barrett retired from his position within a year of the tragedy.

Some twenty years later at Boston Light, Keeper Joshua Bates was taking in borders at the lighthouse to pick up extra cash for himself. He had let out one room to a middle-aged couple named Chardon in the late spring. Mrs. Chardon had been extremely ill and mentally disturbed to the extent that she had lost all memory of her previous life. Yet, for some unknown reason, she had been attracted to Boston Light, so her husband thought living at the light for a few weeks might improve her health and sooth her mind. It seemed, indeed, to have that effect. Mr. Chardon found lighthouse living boring, but his wife walked the rocks in good weather, played in the tidal-pools and often read books, sitting on rocks as close to the sea as she could get. Shag Rocks, less than half a mile away, seemed especially fascinating to her, and she would stare out at the rocks for hours on end. When Keeper Bates asked if she would like to row out to the rocks with him, she shuddered and refused. Mr. Chardon often spent time in the boat with the keeper, although he sometimes hesitated leaving his wife alone on the island. In early summer of 1883, a fifty year old man came to rent the other spare room at the lighthouse from Bates. His name was Edward Moraine, an Englishman. He had been one of the twelve who survived from the wreck of the MARITANA, and had returned to the scene of his near death to meditate. When Moraine met the Chardons at breakfast at the lighthouse, there was an immediate electricity between him and Mrs. Chardon. It was apparent to all present. *"I feel I have met you before,"* she told him. He agreed. He felt the same way, and in fact, knew they had. While Mr. Chardon was out lobstering, fishing or sailing with Keeper Bates, Moraine, although invited to go with them, would remain behind with Mrs. Chardon at the lighthouse. One might think such behavior would make Mr. Chardon jealous, but it had the opposite effect. He could see that her spending time in long conversation and casual walks with Moraine along the rocks of the island, seemed to lift her spirits and make her more aware of the world around her. When a severe gale struck the island a few days later, Mrs. Chardon's mood changed again, but for the worse. As they all remained inside the lighthouse, she began to tremble as the tower did. Her husband tried to calm her, as did Moraine, but she seemed to become more and more fearful. Then she screamed a bone-chilling screech like that of a wounded seagull. She turned to Moraine, her face twisted in pain.

"I know who you are," she shouted for all to hear. *"You are my husband. You were with me, coming from England, and we were torn from each others arms aboard that sinking ship."*

"I know," said Moraine. *"I thought you had drowned that night, and then to find you here was a great shock and yet a great delight at the same time."*

"My name was Alice then," she said, staring at Moraine.

He nodded and reached for her hand. Mr. Chardon just sat, stunned and pale-faced. Mrs. Chardon drew her hand away and sobbing uncontrollably, she ran from the room, dashed down the spiral stairs and ran out into the storm. Most thought she had tripped on the slippery rocks, but others thought a giant wave had caught her unaware. Chardon and Moraine believed it was suicide. Alice's body was found at Shag Rocks, where it was thought she had perished 22 years earlier.

There is even a further irony to this story; the figurehead of the MARITANA, that of a woman carved in wood by a French artisan, bares a strong likeness to Alice Moraine Chardon. The figurehead was originally attached to the bow of the French warship BERCEAU, which was captured by American privateers prior to the War of 1812. It was then the figurehead for the schooner CAROLINE, which wrecked at Boon Island, Maine in 1846. Keeper Nat Baker rescued the crew before the ship sank, but the figurehead floated into York. It was then purchased by Quincy shipbuilders and became the crowning jewel of the square-rigger MARITANA. It was obvious to all who saw the figurehead, but especially to the superstitious Bostonians, that the wood likeness of Alice Moraine Chardon, was a hoodoo, a jinx, another curse connected to Boston Light. Although the MARITANA had been splintered beyond recognition at Shag Rocks, her figurehead was found floating without a scratch in Boston Harbor. It was placed on display for all to see at Boston's Lincoln Wharf, but within days, the wharf mysteriously caught fire. Miraculously, the carving wasn't even scorched. Then placed in Boston's Old State House for safe keeping, the state house too caught on fire. Although many artifacts were destroyed by the flames, the wooden lady once again survived. The figurehead remains on display at the Old State House in downtown Boston; a symbol of all the great tragedies suffered in and around the supposedly cursed Boston Light, America's oldest lighthouse.

The figurehead of the ill-fated MARITANA, wrecked at Boston Light on November 3, 1861, floated into Boston Harbor and is now preserved at Boston's Old State House. It had also been the figurehead of the French warship BERCEAU, captured by privateers, and then the figurehead of the schooner CAROLINE, wrecked at the lighthouse on Boon Island, Maine. It is the likeness of Mrs. Moraine Chardon, a victim aboard the MARITANA.
Courtesy of The Bostonian Society, Old State House, Boston,MA.

Chapter 6
Spirits Of The Shoals

"It is quite impossible to give an idea of these rocky shores – how confusedly they are bound together, lying in all directions: what solid ledges, what great fragments thrown out from the rest. . . as if some of the massive materials of the world remained superfluous after the Creator had finished, and were carelessly thrown down here, where the millionth part of them emerged from the sea, and in the course of thousands of years have become partially bestrewn with a little soil. Pour the blue sea around these islets, and let the surf whitten and steal up from their points, the northwest wind the while raising thousands of whitecaps. . ." These are the words of my fellow Salemite, America's first novelist, Nathaniel Hawthorne, after he first visited the Isles Of Shoals, located ten miles off Portsmouth, New Hampshire. The Isles are just as wondrous and treacherous today as they were when English explorer John Smith stumbled upon them in 1614 and found them *"so remarkable"* that he named them for himself, *"Smith Islands."* The name didn't stick, however, and as early as 1623, when a trading and fishing colony had been established at the Isles, visitor Sir Christopher Levett wrote that, *"The first place I set my foot upon in New England was the Isles Of Shoulds, being islands in the sea about two leagues from the mainland. Upon these islands I neither could see one good timber tree, nor so much ground as to make a garden."* At that time, over 400 men lived at the Isles, but no women were allowed to live there until 1648, when fisherman John Reynolds' wife insisted she move in with him. A court battle ensued, and a reluctant verdict concluded by the members of the Great and General Court of the Massachusetts Bay Colony that, *"if no further complaint come against Mrs. Reynolds, she may enjoy the company of her husband."*

The nine tiny islands surrounded by treacherous shoals and ledges are clustered together and are but barren rocks overgrown with shrubs and thickets, yet they create a yearning, once visited, to return again and again. Mainlander Levi Thaxter, who visited the Isles *"a nervous wreck,"* in July, 1846, wrote on his return to the mainland days later, *"Some of my friends wonder at my excessive affection for the Shoals, and I am surprised to find how much they occupy me."* Levi returned later to marry the lighthouse keeper's daughter.

The nine rocky outcroppings that have inspired unique adventures, romances and mysteries over the centuries, are individually named: Hog or Appledore, Smuttynose, Cedar, Star, Duck, Malaga, White, Seavey and Londoner, which is also called Lunging Island. This latter spit of rock and sand once housed a tavern and trading-post in the early 1600s, and was where mariners came to careen their vessels, to clean and paint the hulls. Among the seamen who frequented the Isles, and especially Lunging Island, were notorious pirates, whom, it seems, the Shoalers welcomed with open arms. Blackbeard, with his fleet of vessels, periodically used the Isles as his base of operations, and the crew of the notorious pirate captain Quelch were actually caught burying gold and silver at the Isles by the Massachusetts Militia. Some pirates, including a few of Captain Kidd's crew, retired to live out their lives on the Isles, one being Philip Babb. *"He is supposed to be so terribly wicked when alive,"* wrote Isles historian Celia Thaxter of Babb, *"that there is no rest for him in his grave."* Says Celia of Babb's ghost, *"He wears a striped butcher's frock with a leather belt, to which is attached a sheath containing a ghostly knife, sharp and glittering, which is his delight to brandish in the face of terrified humanity."* Even one of the dangerous shoal ledges at the Isles is named *"Babb's Rock,"* in fearful respect of that infamous pirate who lived on Appledore. Noted 18th century historian, John Scribner Jenness, writes that, *"there is strong ground for suspicion, indeed, that the Islanders were generally indulgent and sometimes friendly and serviceable in their intercourse with the numerous pirate ships which visited their harbor."*

At the outbreak of the American Revolution, many islanders came to the mainland to live, for fear of British men-o-war attacking their islands, so unprotected and far out to sea. Only a *"ragtag bunch of loose living fishermen"* remained behind on the islands. After the war, a New Hampshire preacher complained to the citizens of Portsmouth that, *"A state of apathetic indolence has failed upon the islanders who appear to have forgotten the world, and whom the world seems to have forgotten, until the condition of poverty and deprivation into which those who remained had lapsed became a matter of public scandal...In some drunken orgie the Shoalsmen had burned their meeting house to the ground. Then for want of a guiding hand, the always looselybound society had fallen into the worst depths of immorality."* Preachers were sent from the coastal towns of Maine, New Hampshire and Massachusetts to civilize the Shoalers and although some progress was made, they remained a fierce, self-reliant and independent people, and a law unto themselves.

Probably one of the most self-reliant Shoalers was Sam Haley, who settled at Smuttynose before the American Revolution. He was not only a fisherman, but he made and sold fish lines and cordage, plus built a tavern from shipwreck lumber and a windmill for grinding grain. He also could be considered the Isles' first lighthouse keeper, for he kept a lantern burning every night in the east window of his home, overlooking the open sea and Cedar Island Ledge, noted for its many shipwrecks.

On the night of a great blizzard, January 14, 1813, Sam Haley's light apparently was not bright enough, for a great Spanish ship hit Cedar Island Ledge on her way out of Portsmouth, New Hampshire and smashed to pieces. In the morning, Haley not only found the surrounding sea littered with timbers, rigging, raisins, almonds and oranges, but with drowned Spanish sailors as well. Three of the Spaniards had actually climbed onto the island during the night, and one had made it to only a few yards from Haley's front door before he froze to death, and Haley had slept through it all. Some thought the ship was the SAGUNTO, which had visited Portsmouth on January 13th to procure a cargo of dried cod, but she successfully sailed out the blizzard and found refuge in Newport. The wrecked ship had supposedly come from Cadiz, Spain, but her name remains a mystery to this day. Fourteen of the Spanish sailors were buried by Haley at Smuttynose, and Spanish pieces-of-eight periodically wash ashore at Appledore and Smuttynose, thought to come from this unknown shipwreck. It was this tragedy that prompted mainlanders to consider building a lighthouse at the Isles Of Shoals, and within seven years, a ninety-foot stone tower with lantern was erected from the rocks of White Island. The island had been named for the family of Whites who had lived there in the 17th and 18th centuries, one member being Captain Joseph White, who, ten years after the lighthouse was built, was the victim of a brutal murder and high society scandal at Salem, Massachusetts. There is not a bit of dirt on the long, rocky White Island, but at low tide it connects with Seavey Island, where some grass does grow, and the lighthouse cow was allowed to graze. Noted poet James Russell Lowell wrote, from his summer retreat at Appledore:

> *"Look southward for White Island light*
> *The lantern stands ninety feet o'er the tide.*
> *There is first a half-mile of tumult and fight*
> *Of dash and roar and tumble and fright*
> *And surging bewilderment wild and wide,*
> *Where the breakers struggle left and right,*
> *Then a mile or more of rushing sea,*
> *And then the lighthouse slim and lone."*

Appropriately, the first keeper of the Isles Of Shoals Light was Sam Haley, Jr., son of old Sam who always kept a light burning in his window. Also appropriately, it was young Sam who uncovered a stash of silver bars while building a sea wall at Cedar Island, thought to possibly be booty left behind by Pirate Quelch and his crew. It was inappropriate, however, that on the night that the ghost of Pirate Philip Babb should visit the lonely lighthouse on White Island, Sam Haley wouldn't be at home. He had gone to 'America,' as Shoalers called the mainland, and left behind a fairly nervous assistant, John Downs, to man the lighthouse. Haley planned to be back before nightfall, but a storm prevented him from leaving Portsmouth by boat. The snowstorm soon turned into an early spring hurricane, and Downs, with his young cousin Peter, were responsible to keep the light shining across the open sea for six nights running.

Pounding breakers constantly shook the lighthouse. John and Peter were not only frightened, but found it all but impossible to sleep, and therefore, they were exhausted as well when dark spirits began to taunt them. In fitful catnaps, as the storm raged around them, young Peter began hallucinating and telling Downs that he saw shadowy figures in the storeroom and in the lantern room, which unnerved Downs to such an extent that he insisted they abandon the lantern room. As they sat in the kitchen below the tower, both almost at their wits' end, there came a rapping at the lighthouse door. It was obvious to them that no one other than themselves could be on the island, and young Peter, hysterical with fear, logically concluded that whoever was knocking at the door was a non-benevolent spirit, and probably Philip Babb in his butcher's cloak, wielding a bloody knife. The knocking continued harder and harder, and there came a moan over the shrieking of the wind and crashing of the waves. John Down was paralyzed with fear, but he knew that he must go to the door and open it. As John grasped the latch and threw the bolt to open the tower to the elements, young Peter protested vehemently. *"Don't do it, please don't do it,"* he pleaded with John, but John flung the door open, and there in the splashing wet and eerie darkness stood a huge hulking black figure. It fell into the room like some ravaging beast. Peter flung himself against the wall and stared in white-eyed fright. At first he couldn't tell what it was – some monster from the sea, he thought, but whatever, he knew it was real, and not a ghost, for it slammed into the table and knocked it over. John Downs knew immediately it was a man, a big black man, half naked, bleeding, and shivering from the cold, but where on earth could he have come from?

John and Peter picked the man off the floor, sat him down and fed him hot coffee and crackers, covering his many cuts and scratches with cloth and bandages. When the man could speak, he told them in a quivering voice that he came off a ship that smashed into the island only a few yards from the lighthouse. It was a Russian brig heading for Salem, loaded with tallow and hides. They had sailed off course in the storm and thought that they were entering Salem Harbor. Fourteen crewmen and the captain remained on board the vessel that was wedged into the rocks, but could break away and sink at any moment. The black crewman had volunteered to jump into the sea, swim to the rocks and climb the island to the lighthouse, which he did, at great peril to himself. Still bleeding profusely, he insisted he return with Peter and John to the shipwreck to help save his crewmates. The wreck was almost directly beneath the lighthouse, but waves smashed over the ship, making rescue operations quite dangerous. Assistant Keeper Downs climbed down into a crevice with a rope tied to his waist, Peter and the black man holding the other end, and he called for the crewmen to jump into the sea as the waves crested and grab for the line, only one at a time so that he could bear their weight as they climbed up the cliff to the two men above. Some were almost swept off the ledge to their death, but after an hour of super-human effort, all aboard were saved and escorted up into the lighthouse for warmth and food. The storm raged for three more days and John Downs feared that they would run out of food, but when the skies cleared, Sam Haley, Jr., arrived at the island with supplies from the mainland. Imagine his surprise when he found his lighthouse filled with Russians. John and Peter were considered heroes of the day, and it was almost fifty years later when John Downs retold his story of the strange nightly visitor to the lighthouse to his grandchildren, that the truth of their fears of ghosts almost prevented them from opening the door that night, which would have meant the deaths of 16 shipwrecked sailors.

It was some ten years after this incident that a new gentle spirit came to the White Island Lighthouse, and one who made the Isles world-renowned. She spoke in whispers and her first impression of the lighthouse was this, when she arrived at "The Rock" on October 11, 1839: *"It was a sunset in autumn that we were set ashore on that loneliest, lovely rock, where the lighthouse looked down on us like some tall, black-capped giant, and filled me with awe and wonder. At its base a few goats were grouped on the rock, standing out dark against the red sky as I looked up at them. The stars were beginning to twinkle; the wind blew cold, charged with the sea's sweetness; the sound of many waters, half bewildered me. Some one began to light the lamps in the tower. Rich, red and golden, they swung round in mid-air; everything was strange and fascinating and new. We entered the quaint little old stone cottage that was for six years our home."*

Celia Laighton was but a child when she went to live on that windswept rock with her father, mother and little brother. Her father, Tom Laighton, had recently been defeated as a candidate for Governor of New Hampshire, which greatly disappointed him, and being appointed lighthouse keeper gave him the lonely retreat he now desired. He swore to his family that he would never set foot on the mainland again, and according to his son Oscar, he was good to his word. *"We had been at White Island seven years,"* writes Oscar Laighton in his book, *"Ninety Years At The Isles Of Shoals,"* and *"father had never returned to Portsmouth,"* but one day a letter came stating that Tom Laighton's brother Joe *"was in some difficulty and sent for him."* Tom launched his little sailboat and headed in toward Portsmouth, some ten miles away. *"We were all watching father"*, writes Oscar, *"and saw him suddenly tack ship when a couple of miles off and head home again. Mother was worried and we all ran to the landing to meet him. Father calmly told us he thought of a way to arrange matters for Uncle Joe, and had determined not to break his vow of never returning to the continent."*

Oscar also writes that, *"although we were marooned on White Island, not hearing from the continent sometimes for weeks, my mother became fond of our storm-swept ion' of rock in midocean, not much larger than a good-sized ship. She told me later that the winter on the island, in a fearful gale of wind from the northeast, the boat houses were washed off with all father's boats and the long walk leading up to the light was carried away, and nothing was left but the dwelling, which was built of stone, and the light tower. Father had a flock of hens, and they were lost with the boats. This was the storm when the ship POCAHONTAS was lost with all hands. My sister tells about this in her poem, 'The Wreck Of The POCAHONTAS.' She heard, with mother, the signal guns from the doomed ship, as she went past our light."*

Writes young Celia:

"I lit the lamps in the lighthouse tower, for the sun dropped down and the day was dead. They shone like a glorious clustered flower, – Ten golden and five red.

Looking across, where the line of coast stretched darkly, shrinking away from the sea, the lights sprang out at the edge, – almost they seemed to answer me!

O warning lights! burn bright and clear, hither the storm comes! Leagues away it moans and thunders low and drear, – Burn till the break of day!

A mournful breeze began to blow; Weird music it drew through the iron bars; The sullen billows boiled below, and dimly 'peared the stars.

The sails that flecked the ocean floor from east to west leaned low and fled; They knew what came in the distant roar that filled the air with dread!

Flung by a fitful gust, there beat against the window a dash of rain; Steady as a tramp of marching feet strode on the hurricane.

It smote the waves for a moment still, level and deadly white for fear; the bare rock shuddered, – an awful thrill shook even my tower of cheer.

Like all the demons loosed at last, whistling and shrieking, wild and wide, the mad wind raged, while strong and fast rolled in the rising tide. . .

When morning dawned, above the din of gale and breaker boomed a gun! Another! We who sat within answered with cries each one.

Into each other's eyes with fear We looked through helpless tears, as still, one after one, near and more near, the signals pealed, until

The thick storm seemed to break apart to show us, staggering to her grave, the fated brig.. We had no heart to look, for naught could save.

*One glimpse of black hull heaving slow, then closed the mists
o'er canvas torn and tangled ropes swept to and from masts
that raked forlorn.*

*We told our tale, and the boatman cried: 'Twas the
'Pocahontas,' – all were lost! For miles along the coast the
tide her shattered timbers tossed."*

*Then I looked the whole horizon round, – So beautiful the
ocean spread about us, o'er those sailors drowned! "Father
in heaven," I said, –*

*And I shut the beauty from my sight, for I thought of the dead
that lay below; From the bright air faded the warmth and
light, there came a chill like snow.*

*Sighing I climbed the lighthouse stair, half forgetting my grief
and pain; And while the day died, sweet and fair, I lit the
lamps again."*

Celia had only been at the lighthouse a few weeks when the POCAHONTAS wrecked. In her autobiography, she writes, *"We were startled by the heavy booming of the guns through the roar of the tempest, – a sound that drew nearer and nearer, till at last, through a sudden break in the mist and spray, we saw the heavily rolling hull of a large vessel driving by, to her sure destruction, toward the coast. It was as if the wind had torn the vapor apart on purpose to show us the piteous sight; and I well remember a hand on my shoulder which held me firmly , shuddering child that I was, and forced me to look in spite of myself. What a day of pain it was! How dread the sound of those signal guns and how much more dread the certainty when they ceased, that all was over! We learned afterward that it was the brig POCAHONTAS, homeward bound from Spain, and that the vessel and her crew were lost."*

Strangely, Celia doesn't mention that her uncle, Mark Laighton, was the helmsman of the POCAHONTAS only a year before the disaster. Noted author Richard Henry Dana, in his *"Two Years Before The Mast,"* states that, *"No danger on the ship with Mark Laighton at the wheel,"* which certainly attests to his navigational abilities, but one wonders, why wasn't he at the helm on that fateful morning in December of 1839? Some historians believe that lighthouse keeper Thomas Laighton thought he was, when he and Celia spotted the floating wreck pass by them on that foggy morning, but that he didn't want to further frighten his daughter with his fears that Uncle Mark was aboard and about to meet his doom. Dana's book on *"the life of a common sailor at sea as it really is,"* was published a year after the shipwreck, and became an immediate best seller. Celia mentions at the time, *"That was the last word that ever reached us about Mark."* Presumably, Mark was lost at sea, and ironically his last known duty was aboard the POCAHONTAS.

Celia's poem was a phenomenal success, and prompted the editor of the *Atlantic Monthly*, the leading magazine of the day, to persuade her to write more about her island home. Celia's prose and poetry about the Isles Of Shoals brought new visitors to these Isles of wonder, including such notables as Henry David Thoreau, Nathaniel Hawthorne, James Russell Lowell, Richard Dana, Edward Everet Hale and the Longfellows, and they continued to return summer after summer, along with other bluebloods of Boston, who discovered the Isles through Celia's writings. The greatest surprise to all, however, was their initial meetings with Celia Laighton, for she was younger than they all expected, more beautiful than imagined, and as sweet and innocent as her soft poetic words. All who met her fell in love with her. As one Shoals historian, Lyman Rutledge, explains her charm and beauty, *"because she was intimate with the dancing waves, the laughing sky, the rising sun, the soaring gulls and every living thing. The abundance of her own life, the keenness of all her perceptions, the full response of her nature to the greatness of nature around her made every object glow as if possessed of some inner illumination. . . It was all so much a part of her that she must 'speak these things that made life so sweet."*

One young suitor who came often to the lighthouse to visit, was a cousin, Christopher Rhymes. He was sixteen, but Celia was only twelve. Rhymes was an inventor of sorts, and besides having a crush on Celia, he was obsessed with the island's only cow, Bessie. When a storm was brewing, Bessie was led into the kitchen to live with the family until the storm subsided, and in all respects, Bessie was treated more like a pet or member of the family than the island's provider of milk, cream, cheese and butter. Since Celia didn't like the long, tedious chore of churning to make butter, Rymes built a windmill out of driftwood and attached it to the butter churner, so that butter could be made by wind power. Although it was noisy, Rymes' invention worked well, until, as Oscar tells it, *"the cow was attracted by the noise and came on deck to investigate. No one will know what thoughts rushed through her mind. She evidently considered the mill was something to be dealt with promptly, for she suddenly lowered her head and charged, smashing the fans, knocking over the churn and wrecking the whole outfit."*

Another older man who was interested in young Celia was Levi Lincoln Thaxter. He visited the lighthouse by boat one day and found it too stormy to leave the island, so Tom Laighton took him in to stay a few days at the lighthouse – an act of kindness that he soon regretted, for Levi, a bearded twenty-four year old graduate of Harvard, fell head-over-heels in love with 13 year old Celia. Levi proposed marriage and Tom Laighton flew into a rage, ordering Levi off the island. Levi stood up to Celia's father, and although he left the island in a huff, he threatened to build a hut at the Isles and live in it until Celia was old enough to speak for herself. Levi was true to his word. He built a bachelor's cottage at Appledore Island, just about the time Tom Laighton left the lighthouse service and built a tourist hotel at Appledore. Levi ate his meals at the hotel for two years in the summer, and left the Isles in the winter to return to his home in Watertown, Massachusetts. During one early November departure, Tom Laighton wrote in his Journal: *"Levi went home to Watertown and was sick, and I was sick for several days after his departure myself."* At age 15, Celia was enrolled at the Mount Washington Seminary for girls at South Boston, and Thomas finally consented to the wedding of Levi and Celia, if Levi would wait twelve months. Sam Longfellow, brother of poet Henry, wrote home to mother, *"Levi is bethrothed to Celia Laighton, the daughter of him who once kept the lighthouse and now keeps the hotel – a simple, frank and pleasing girl of fifteen, who has grown up on the Islands, the flower of the rocks."* The bluebloods of Boston were shocked, but neither Levi nor Celia cared a bit of what they thought – they would live out their lives at the Isles, carefree and content – and Celia continued to write her simple masterpieces. As Rutledge concludes, *"Nothing finer has fallen from Celia's pen than her memories of childhood in the shadow of the lighthouse."* She thrived at the Isles and created a new wholesome and loving spirit there – *"This solemn gray lid was lifted at its western edge, and an insufferable splendor screamed across the world from the sinking sun. The whole heaven was in a blaze of scarlet, across which sprang a rainbow unbroken to the topmost clouds – the sea answered the sky's rich blush, and the gray rocks drowned the melancholy purple. I hid my face from the glory – it was too much to bear."* – Celia Laighton Thaxter.

Celia Thaxter and her beloved White Island Light at The Isles Of Shoals, New Hampshire.
Sketch from Harper's Magazine.

Fastnet Rock Lighthouse, twelve miles off Cork, Ireland, is considered the most dangerous place for vessels by the Irish. They call it, "the teardrop of Ireland."

The Eddystone Light off Plymouth, England, as it stands today, with the base of one of the old, 1759 lighthouse, behind it. The first Eddystone toppled with the designer-builder inside it in 1703.

The remains of the Old Head of Kinsale Lighthouse, Ireland.

The ANNIE C. MCGUIRE wrecks at Portland Head Light on Christmas Eve, 1886, with the local sheriff waiting in the lighthouse to arrest her commander.
An 1886 photo, courtesy Maine Historical Society.

Chapter 7
Graveyard of the North

Along all the wind-swept rugged coastlines of the Atlantic, fishermen and mariners are quick to claim their own little watery territory as the most treacherous. One might think that sea travelers would be reluctant to claim their waters as the most dangerous and uninviting, but there seems to be a grim pride in labeling home waters as *"Graveyard of the Atlantic."* Newfoundland and Nova Scotia both make claim to it, as does Maine, Cape Cod, Nantucket, Rhode Island, New York, New Jersey and Cape Hatteras, not to mention West England, Ireland and Scotland. Even France, especially off Brittany and Normandy, considers its stormy seas the most perilous. Possibly at any one time in history, one area claim might be more valid than another. A sudden hurricane or blizzard can quickly increase maritime hazards in a specific coastal territory, or even a persistent fog or sea mist, frost or pack ice can enhance the danger to vessels traveling in the area. Possibly, one might decide that where you find the most lighthouses would be the most treacherous waters, but some lighthouses were erected to guide vessels successfully into harbors of busy ports, rather than to mark reefs and shoals. Incidence and intensity of disasters at lighthouses might, however, be justifiable in claiming the surrounding sea as being the *"Graveyard of the North Atlantic."*

Fourteen miles south-west of the harbor of Plymouth, England is a notorious reef of red rock, stretching underwater at high tide for some six hundred yards. It is known as Eddystone, plagued by swift and erratic currents and the full force of a west wind. It is a dangerous place for ships to pass, and yet they must come close to Eddystone to get in and out of England's famous and active harbor. Mariners and merchants persuaded the King and Queen, William and Mary, in 1694, to allow a lighthouse to be built at Eddystone with private funds. All qualified architects in the country considered the building of such a structure in open water a great folly, and all refused to participate. Finally, an eccentric inventor named Henry Winstanley took up the challenge. He had once owned two vessels that wrecked at Eddystone, and he was determined to build a solid structure that would withstand the worst of storms. Local businessmen said it couldn't be done, which made him all the more determined. After four years of work and many setbacks, the lighthouse was completed in 1699. When the candles were lit by Winstanley himself to illuminate the reef, the people on shore celebrated, but the builder and his assistants could not, for a wild storm kept them at the lighthouse for eleven days. The structure shuddered as each wave struck the reef, so Winstanley made iron hoops to wrap around its cement base for strength, and increased the tower's height to 80 feet above sea level. To calm the fears of his investors, some of whom felt the lighthouse wouldn't stand the pounding of constant winter storms, Winstanley publicly proclaimed that, *"I ask nothing better than to be inside the lighthouse dur-*

ing the greatest storm that ever was." It was not just a great storm, it was the greatest storm in British history, and only by coincidence, Henry Winstanley happened to be aboard his lighthouse. It hit on the evening of November 26, 1703, and Winstanley was in the lighthouse making a few minor repairs. Unfortunately, he decided to stay the night. Almost 1,000 homes were lost in the West of England that night, 400 windmills were blown down, 600 churches lost roofs, 150 ships were sunk, with 8,000 sailors killed. When the storm subsided and the people of Plymouth looked to sea, their lighthouse was gone, with Winstanley in it. The inventor was granted his final wish, to be inside the lighthouse during the greatest storm ever.

From that moment on, Eddystone became one of the most notorious places of danger in the world. Three lighthouses have been built on the red reef since Winstanley's self-made coffin. A replacement in 1709, which stood for 47 years and was destroyed by fire, a stone structure in 1759, which the sea undermined, and the tower of today, which was built in 1882. All were monuments to Henry Winstanley, the first man who thought it could be done and he did it. The Eddystone Light has been a symbol of hope and endurance in England for centuries, and the subject of famous folktales, poems and songs.

Another graveyard of ships, long considered by the British as one of the most treacherous, is called "The Smalls." It consists of twenty rugged islets located twenty miles off the English coast. The islets had been the cause of so many shipwrecks, that leader of the Liverpool dock-workers, John Phillips, was determined to build a lighthouse on the tallest islet in 1773. The workers built an octagonal structure 22-feet in diameter and 70-feet above the high water mark, made of cast iron and oak. With much rehab and repairs over the years, the Smalls Lighthouse lasted over 80 years. Two keepers were placed on permanent duty at the light. Both were from the village of Solva, and strangely, they were men who hated each other, and whose families had been enemies for as far back as anyone could remember. Yet, they agreed to be fellow keepers of the light.

Over the first winter it was so stormy that food and supplies were delayed for weeks because the supply ship could not land at the islet. After being forced back to the mainland without making their delivery, the supply-boat personnel reported that one of the keepers stood at the base of the lighthouse on the rocks waving continuously while being deluged by icy waves, and the other keeper in the lantern gallery kept the lantern glowing, yet flew a distress flag. Weeks later, with a slight calming of the seas, a local fisherman managed to beach his small boat at the lighthouse and carried both keepers back to the mainland. One had gone insane and the other was a corpse. It was determined by the authorities that one had died from the fever early in the winter. Although, for sanitary reasons, the corpse couldn't remain inside the lighthouse for weeks as the storm raged, the keeper dare not bury his dead companion at sea, for fear that the mainlanders would think he murdered his old enemy. The only way he could prove that he didn't kill his co-keeper was to preserve the body so that the authorities could see he died of natural causes and not from foul play. The surviving keeper built a wooden coffin and lashed it in an upright position to the base of the lighthouse. As waves splashed in, the corpse's arm moved with the splashing sea, giving the impression that he was waving to passing ships. From that day until The Small Lighthouse was automated, three keepers were appointed to always be on duty together at all times, and it soon became the law of all British lighthouses.

Ireland also has its "Graveyard of a Thousand Ships," off the south and west coasts, from Old Head of Kinsale Lighthouse, where the LUSITANIA went under in 1915, to Inishtrahull Light, County Donegal, at the northern tip of the country, where the Atlantic meets the Irish sea. The remote Inishtrahull Lighthouse was built in 1813 by a group of men, some of whom met disaster while building another lighthouse on the south coast that same year. The 24 men building the lighthouse base at Tuskar Rock, were swept away by a heavy sea, half of them drowning. Sixty miles from Old Head of Kinsale Light, stands another lonely islet, looking in size and shape of a ship under full sail, twelve miles off the mainland of Cork. Riding 90 feet out of the sea, it is called Fastnet Rock and is considered by Irishmen as the most dangerous place in the world for vessels. It is also known by locals as, "The Tear-drop of Ireland," for it was the last bit of land seen by those leaving Ireland for America during the potato famine of the mid 1800s. Adding to the wild waves and thick fog, fierce tidal currents and twelve foot tides, have caused many vessels to smash into Fastnet Rock. The decision to build a lighthouse on the lonely rock came in 1847, when the American passenger ship STEPHEN WHITNEY wrecked there, with 100 lives lost. An 83-foot oil burning lighthouse was built at Fastnet, completed in 1854, but in rough weather, which occurred quite fre-quently, the tower *"trembled like a leaf,"* reported the keeper, *"and tea on tables at the top of the tower, pitched to the floor."* Three-ton rocks from the base of the tower began to dislodge. Repairs were made, but an 1881 storm almost toppled the light and permanently damaged the lantern lens. It was decided then to build a completely new lighthouse at Fastnet Rock. This time it was to be stronger and taller, to a height of 176 feet. It was completed in June of 1904 and was automated in 1989 – it continues to be the shining eye of Europe for transatlantic voyagers from the Americas.

Two other island groupings considered a great danger to vessels traveling off the West coast of Ireland, are the Skelligs off County Kerry, and 22 miles north of Great and Little Skellig, are the six islands and islets called The Blaskets, off the tip of the Dingle Peninsula. These islands, many looking more like the peaks of mountains rather than islands, are surrounded by strong cur-rents and are noted for *"capsizing swells,"* even on calm weather days. They are also all quite impossible to land on in rough seas. Some were once the homes of Irish monks dating back over 1,000 years. The peak of Great Skeelig, 700 feet above the sea, and Great Blasket Island, still retain the buildings from ancient monastic communities. Many vessels from the fleeing Spanish Armada of 1588 met disaster in the churning waters around the Skelligs and the Blaskets, as have many ships since. An estimated 29 Spanish ships sank off Ireland in storms in that one year after the Armada suffered defeat by the English and tried to return to Spain by circling the Emerald Isle.

Two lighthouses were built at Great Skellig in 1825, one at 175-feet and the other on the high cliffs at 375-feet. There was no water on the island and derricks were built to lift food, water and fuel from vessels to the lighthouses, and as slings to lift keepers and their families on and off the island. Landing on the island from a boat for most of the year was impossible. The families brought rabbits for food because there was little grass for sheep or cows to graze. The rabbits soon multiplied until they swarmed over the island and ferrets had to be brought in to consume them all. Life on the mountainous island was extremely dangerous for the children of the keepers and at least three were killed falling off high cliffs, as was one keeper, Michael Wiseheart, who had been a survivor of the Tuskar Rock tragedy. He slipped and fell some 375 feet off Great Skellig while he was trying to mow a small patch of grass around the lighthouse.

Because of the remoteness, loneliness and harassing weather, petty arguments periodically erupted, causing friction between the keeper of the lower light and the keeper of the upper light. This climaxed in the winter of 1865, when an intoxicated lower keeper visited the upper keeper and beat him up, *"to an inch of his life."* The lower keeper lost his job and his light was converted into a fog signal station, and the upper lighthouse was removed entirely. It was replaced by a new lighthouse on the Blaskets and was built on Inishtearaght, the island furthest from the mainland, which rises 600-feet above sea level like a foreboding black fortress of stone. Although once occupied by fishermen, only a keeper and some sheep remain on this island. The advent of the light reduced the number of vessels that wrecked on the island, thus spoiling a lucrative wrecking livelihood for the island villagers, which eventually forced them to move to the mainland to survive. Great rogue waves often smash into this lighthouse called Tearacht, building up in mid ocean and gaining height and power until they reach the outer island. One such wave flooded the lantern room in 1951, 175-feet above the sea. Such a giant, destructive wave is good reason, think Irish mariners, if no other, to dub Western Ireland as *"The Graveyard of the North Atlantic,"* with a stretch of some 3,000 miles of the wildest and windiest seas until one reaches America.

Down East Maine, like neighboring Nova Scotia, can add an extra menacing element to their Atlantic graveyards that is not predominant in the wild seas of Britain and Ireland – that is ice. There are many disasters in the freezing waters of Maine caused by the icing of ships and the freezing of people as there are tragedies of wind and wave, or shipwrecks and collisions caused by fog. The most memorable being a schooner freezing to the rocks at Owl Head at the entrance to Rockland Harbor, at the foot of the lighthouse, in December of 1850. Although there were five other vessels aground near the brick lighthouse during this pre-Christmas blizzard, Keeper William Masters considered the little schooner that had drifted across the bay from Jameson's Point to be in the greatest peril. She had plowed into the rocks, punctured her hull and was taking in water as icy waves sprayed over her from the bow-spirit. The tide was coming and there was no way for the two men and woman who occupied the schooner to get ashore. Their wet clothes were freezing to their bodies and they could not escape the bone-numbing cold. Night was coming on, the wind was rising as the temperature plummeted. For crewmen Roger Elliot and Dick Ingraham, with Ingraham's fiancée Lydia Dyer, there seemed no escape of either drowning or freezing to death. They decided to lay on deck, one on top of the other and wrap the only two wet blankets they had around their bodies. Soon, with waves spraying over them they became one solid block of ice, but the schooner did not sink. All fell into a deep frozen sleep, but Elliott, kept picking at the ice that covered them to allow fresh air into their frozen cocoon.

At dawn, the tide was out, and Elliott, with stiffened clothes and aching joints, managed to break the six inch thick ice pack holding him to the others and slide off the deck to the rocks below. The others, Elliott noted, had turned blue and were not breathing – they hugged each other in a frozen grip. When Elliott tried to walk he tumbled over backwards, and found he couldn't stand, so he crawled through snow up the rocks, through a large snowdrift to the road. There were hoof-prints in the snow, and in agony, he followed the horse tracks, which led him to Owl Head Lighthouse. He rang the bell for help and Keeper Masters dragged Elliott inside and thawed him out before the fireplace. After a couple of jiggers of rum, Elliott could talk. He told the keeper about the other two aboard the schooner, and then he once again drifted off into deep sleep. He woke again to hear the loud clanging of the lighthouse emergency bell. Keeper Masters was summoning help from the village. Soon, there were a dozen or so men backtracking Elliott's footprints to the rocks and splintered schooner. The tide was coming in again, but the men waded into the water waist deep to get across to the frozen couple. Instead of trying to thaw them, the men lifted the heavy cake of ice that contained the two bodies, carried it ashore and set it in a wagon. Although all the men present concluded that the couple was dead, they drove the wagon to the lighthouse, and there in the kitchen before the fire began chipping away at the ice. When the frozen blankets were removed from them, the women folk who had now arrived at the lighthouse began massaging the stiff bodies. After almost an hour of praying and rubbing her skin, Lydia began to stir slightly. Within another hour she was conscious and Dick

Ingraham also began showing signs of returning to life. All those present had been convinced that the couple had frozen to death, and now they were witnessing a miracle – it was surely intervention from heaven that had brought them back to life, they concluded. Within a few weeks the couple was restored to perfect health, yet Roger Elliott, the true hero of the drama, continued to suffer physical pain and mental trauma throughout his life, due to the ordeal aboard the schooner. Lydia and Dick were soon married and over many happy years, produced four children. Their miraculous recovery, however, is still the subject of controversy with the old salts of Maine and cause of constant debate around bait-barrels. Were they or were they not dead when thawed out in the kitchen of the Owl Head Lighthouse?

The folks of Maine, although superstitious, don't take to believing in miracles that easily, and when it seemed another had occurred at Owl Head Light years after the frozen couple came back to life, they came to ponder the possibility that maybe the lighthouse itself was especially blessed. The second miracle concerned the mail-boats that deliver newspapers, mail and other supplies to the island inhabitants and lighthouse keepers. This is a dangerous business, especially in the winter. Rockland Harbor is sometimes filled with ice, and such was the case in 1920, when the mail-boat coming into Owl Head could not enter the harbor because it was frozen over. The three young men aboard the boat decided not to even attempt to break through the ice, which could possibly cut a hole through the hull, and they headed back out to sea in an attempt to make Matinicus Island. Neither the mail-boat, nor her three occupants were ever seen again. The mail-stacks they were to deliver, however, were discovered drifting all along the coast of Maine over the entire winter. A few years later, another mail-boat was coming into Rockland, and this time it wasn't ice, but fog that blocked their way. Add to the fog; snow, sleet and zero visibility, and the mail-boat skipper lost his bearings. He kept blaring his steam-whistle, hoping to hear a response from the fog-bell at the lighthouse, but the wind was howling as well, and as much as the skipper and crew strained their ears, they heard no bell. The mail-boat was hopelessly lost in dangerous waters. They did however, soon hear the faint sound of a dog barking over the wind, which alerted them that they were heading into a rocky coast. The skipper spun the wheel, quickly changing his course, missing Owl Head reef by only a few feet. The men aboard had recognized the bark of the dog as coming from Spot, the lighthouse keeper's pet spaniel. Spot was noted by local fishermen and mariners for ringing the fog-bell during thick weather, a trick taught to it by it's master. This night however, Spot had been inside the keeper's house at the feet of his master in front of a hot stove, but the dog scratched at the door in the midst of the storm and was let out of doors, the keeper thought, to relieve its kidney. Spot had apparently heard the mail-boat steam-whistle and had attempted to ring the fog-bell located on the high cliff, by yanking the clapper-bell rope with its teeth, but the bell was deeply covered with snow, which produced only a muffled bonging sound. Spot realized that the sound was not loud enough to warn the mail-boat from the rocks, and using good old Yankee inginuity, began barking loud enough for the mail-boat crew to heed the warning. It wasn't until the mail-boat skipper phoned the lighthouse from Rockland to thank the keeper, that the keeper realized what Spot had done. When calmer weather prevailed, Spot was delivered a steak from the mail-boat skipper, and a medal for its collar proclaiming the little spaniel a genuine life saving hero.

Wood Island Light located south of Portland, Maine, also had a dog named Sailor in the mid 1940s that rang the fog-bell in misty or stormy weather. Like Spot, Sailor would pull on the clapper-cord with its strong canine teeth until the passing vessels would respond with a toot on the ship's whistle or rang the ship's bell in response. It soon became tradition that seamen coming in and out of Saco Bay would signal Sailor with a bell or whistle in foul weather and fair, to watch the poor dog scurry for the fog-bell to respond until they drove it insane. Prior to Sailor, Wood Island was notorious for shipwrecks, and even after the lighthouse was established there in 1808, the island averaged four shipwrecks per year. A most bizarre tragedy occurred in the area when three vessels wrecked on the same day, March 3, 1947. In a fierce storm, the steamer NOVODOC, the collier ALEXANDER and the dragger PEMAQUID all met their doom with a total of 24 lives lost. The most remarkable unwanted visitor to the rocks at Wood Island Light was the QUEEN OF THE WEST, a schooner that seemed determined to wreck there. Under command of Captain J. Greenlaw, she hit the ledge surrounding the lighthouse on October 14, 1898, and although heavily damaged, she was salvaged. Exactly 43 days later, she drove into the ledge again, very near where she had wrecked before, but this time she went to pieces. The keeper did, however, manage to save all of her occupants.

Neither Owl Head Light nor Wood Island Light are located at what is considered the most perilous places along the rocky Maine coast. Mount Desert Rock Light, located twenty miles to sea from Mount Desert Island, is conceivably Maine's most remote lighthouse and experiences the roughest of weather. The lighthouse was built high on a seaside cliff in 1830, and a storm twelve years later, so the keeper's log reveals, displaced a 54-ton rock from one end of the 100-yard long island to the other. In one vicious storm, quotes the keeper, *"the boathouse washed off the rock and circled the island twice and a big sea landed it right back on the island beside the tower. The very next sea hit the hen house and washed it off too. For awhile, we thought it was going to come back and land, but it didn't. It drifted off, hens and all."*

Although Maine mariners might argue over which of the state's seventy or so lighthouses sit overlooking the most jeopardous of seas and experience the most violent weather, Matinicus Rock Light would be near the top of all their lists. It is one of the world's most isolated stations, located on a thirty-acre barren outcropping of rocks, twenty miles to sea from the mainland, and four miles from Matinicus Island. Two wooden lighthouse towers were built there in 1827, and both were washed away in a storm twenty years later. The old keeper who lived through the tempest was not willing to keep two stone lighthouses that were erected there soon after, and a mainlander named Sam Burgess took the job, moving his family to the rock in 1853. Supplies were delivered to the rock only twice a year, and in 1856, the supplies did not arrive on schedule, forcing Keeper Burgess to row to Matinicus Island for needed food and medicine. He left behind his sickly wife and sixteen-year old daughter Abbie to tend to the lighthouse in his absence. Abbie and her invalid mother were alone at the lighthouse for almost one month, due to rough seas, and she later wrote to a childhood friend of her experiences:

"You have often expressed a desire to view the sea out upon the ocean when it is angry. Had you been here on January 19, I surmise you would have been satisfied. Father was away. Early in the day, as the tide rose, the sea made a complete breach over the rock, washing every movable thing away, and of the old dwelling not one stone was left upon another of the foundation. The new dwelling was flooded and the shutters had to be secured to prevent the violence of the spray from breaking them in. As the tide came, the sea rose higher and higher, till the only endurable places were the light towers. If they stood we were saved, otherwise our fate was only too certain. But for some reason, I know not why, I had no misgivings and went on with my work as usual. For four weeks, owing to rough weather, no landing could be made on the rock."

Caring for her mother and younger siblings, Abbie Burgess weathered the storm and kept the twin lights burning all the time her father was away and unable to return. When, for political reasons, her father lost his job as keeper in 1860, Abbie stayed on at Matinicus Rock Light to help the novice new keeper. Soon, she fell in love with the new keeper's son, Issac Grant. They were eventually married, and Abbie Burgess Grant went on to keep lighthouses with her husband in Maine until 1905.

An American medal of gold was awarded to Lighthouse Keeper Marcus Hanna in 1885, for *"single heroism involving great peril."* Yet, only moments before his "courageous heroism," he was sick in bed with pneumonia at the Cape Elizabeth Lighthouse station. His wife, who was caring for the lanterns, happened to look out the window to see a schooner in distress on the rocks below. She reluctantly woke her husband. The keeper was soon up, dressed and *"out into one of the coldest days and most violent snowstorm I have ever witnessed,"* he later reported, *"with snow drifts three to five feet high."* The foundering schooner was the AUSTRALIA out of Boothbay, bound for Boston. Her mainsail had ripped and blown away, leaving the vessel helpless and she drifted in to smash onto the rocks. There were three men aboard who were crying for help and had no means of getting ashore. The schooner was breaking up. The temperature was below zero and the wind was howling at eighty miles an hour, carrying snow and sleet that stung the face. Marcus Hanna realized that the men would surely drown or freeze to death within the hour without help from shore. Reaching the slippery ice covered rocks, Hanna attempted to throw them a lifeline, but the line couldn't reach them. Suddenly, a large wave pushed the schooner further in and Hanna's line was finally caught by one of the crewmen, but his hands were so numb with cold that he couldn't tie the line to anything aboard. Hanna then waded waist deep into the frigid water, shouting to the crewmen to tie the line to his waist and jump overboard so Hanna could haul him inshore. One crewman managed to get the rope around his waist, loop it to his belt and Hanna hauled him off the deck and managed to pull the shivering battered man to the rocks and drag him away from the spray. By this time, Mrs. Hanna had raised the distress flag and ran to the nearest house to get help. Rescuers began arriving on the scene. The keeper entered the pounding surf again and threw the line to a second crewman who was shivering uncontrollably. *"He was a helpless frozen lump of humanity,"* Hanna commented later. With the help of his neighbors, the keeper managed to haul this man ashore as well. The crewman was so frozen that he had gone blind. *"His whole appearance was ghastly,"* said Hanna. Still waist deep in water, the keeper managed to throw the line to the skipper who was still aboard, but unable to move. Before Hanna could save him, a large wave knocked him into the frothing sea; and when he washed ashore hours later, he was dead. *"I never knew where I got the energy to save those two crewmen,"* Hanna said later, *"but I wish I could have saved Captain Lewis as well."* The snowdrifts were so high that the rescuers and the victims could not make it to the lighthouse and had to find shelter in the fog-signal station. Two days later, the crewmen and Keeper Hanna were taken from the signal station to the hospital, where all survived, and the blind crewmen regained his sight. The tough old keeper was soon back to his duties and justifiably awarded the nation's highest civilian award for heroism.

Around Cape Elizabeth and heading into Portland Harbor, Maine's busiest port, is the light at Portland Head, built in 1787. It is the most photographed, painted and advertised lighthouse in Maine, and possibly the world. It is constantly visited by tourists. Keeper Earle Benson's wife recalled that, *"Once a lady walked right into our keeper's quarters, sat at the kitchen table and demanded that I wait on her. I told her that this was my home, but she said that I was a government employee and she expected to be served."*

Probably the greatest attraction ever at Portland Head Light was Keeper Prout's intelligent and talkative parrot Billy, who was constantly on duty in the early 1900s. He had the language of a pirate, and a few chosen words from Billy often sent snooping tourists scampering away. Billy was also a living barometer and often told the keeper when to expect a storm, or to *"Turn on the horn Zeb, it's getting foggy."* The parrot once saved a young boy's life when he spotted him falling off the rocks surrounding the lighthouse and being swept to sea. Billy set up such a ruckus of screeching and cursing that Zeb Prout knew that the bird was unduly disturbed, and searching the surf, he spotted the drowning boy and jumped in to save him.

The waters off Cape Elizabeth and Portland Head can be as rough and treacherous as any Maine waters, and probably the most unique shipwreck story at Portland Head is that of ANNIE C. MAGUIRE. She was heading into Portland on a snowy Christmas Eve, 1886. Waiting to see if the ship was heading in, hiding at the lighthouse, was the county sheriff. He held a warrant to arrest the ship's commander, Captain O'Neil, who was wanted in other counties for running out without paying some hefty bills. The sheriff suspected that if O'Neil spotted him, he might head out to sea again, so imagine the sheriff's surprise when O'Neil landed directly at his feet. Blinded by the snowstorm, O'Neil drove his ship onto the rocks at Portland Head Light. The keeper with a rescue party, saved all the ship's company, including O'Neil. The minute the commander stepped ashore, the sheriff served him with the summons. *"But all my worldly goods are aboard the wrecked vessel,"* said the surprised O'Neil, *"therefore I can't pay these bills."* *"Not so,"* spoke up O'Neils' wife, *"I placed all our money in my hat-box, which I carried ashore, and it is safe."* The sheriff couldn't have been more pleased.

Another bizarre shipwreck occurred off Portland Head Light on February 4, 1864. The steamer BOHEMIAN coming from Liverpool, England with 317 people aboard, smashed into Alden Rock, Cape Elizabeth in a dense fog. The ship filled quickly with water and some lifeboats were launched before she went under, but many passengers panicked and some lifeboats were launched with only a few people in them. The captain ordered many of the rowers to return to the sinking ship for more passengers, but most refused and headed in for the lighthouse. The captain continuously sent up emergency flares, but no help came from shore. The lighthouse keeper was unaware that the BOHEMIAN was sinking. It happened to be Washington's Birthday, always celebrated with fireworks displays in those days. The emergency flares were considered to be part of the holiday celebration. Because of the rescue delay form shore, over forty passengers from the BOHEMIAN drowned.

Some sixty miles south as the gull flies, from Portland to Cape Cod, Massachusetts, hard rock turns to sand along the shore, but sailors consider these seas at this great hook of sand as hazardous as Maine's. Although the Gulf Stream travels up the outside coast of the Cape, often keeping the shore clear of snow and ice, cold and treacherous offshore sandbars are added factors of fear for the mariners. Governor Bradford of Plymouth Plantation in 1620, writes: •

"A word or two by ye way of this Cape: It was first named by Captain Gosnold and his company in 1602; but it retains ye former name amongst seamen, also ye extreme point which first showed those dangerous shouls unto them, called Point Care and Tucker's Terror – named by Capt. Gosnold on account of the expressed fears of one of his company-but ye French and Dutch, to this day, call it Malabarr, by reason of those perilous Shouls, and ye losses they have suffered there."

The Cape Cod Lighthouse, also called Highland Light, was built ten years after the Portland Head Light in 1797, on a 125-foot high clay dune facing the sea at Truro, near the tip of the Cape, *"to prevent many fatal accidents."* It became a flashing beacon so navigators would not mistake it for the steady Boston Light, and the first to operate it was Issac Small, the first of many in the Small family who, through two centuries dedicated their lives to the lighthouse service. One constant visitor to the light was famed author and naturalist Henry David Thoreau, who, in his journal remarked that, *"The keeper must keep an account of the number of vessels which pass his light during the day, but there are hundreds of vessels in sight at once, steering in all directions, many on the very verge of the horizon, and he must have more eyes than Argus, and be a good deal farther sighted."*

Another noted author and historian, Samuel Adams Drake, tells us that in the winter of 1874-75, the extreme cold blocked up a number of New England Harbors, including Provincetown and Truro. *"Provincetown, that is so providentially situated to receive the storm-tossed mariner, was hermetically sealed by a vast ice-field, which extended from Wood End to Monomet, a distance of twenty-two miles. In the neighborhood of Provincetown a fleet of fishing vessels that was unable to reach the harbor became immovably imbedded in the floe thus realizing at our very doors all the perils of Arctic navigation. Flags of distress were displayed in every direction from the masts of crippled vessels that no help could reach. Some of these luckless craft were crushed and sunk to the bottom, others were abandoned by their crews. It would not be extravagant to say that the beach on the ocean-side, between Highland Light and Wood End, was strewed with wrecks. The saddest of all was one from Palerma, a terrible gale, which tore the frozen sails in shreds from her masts, drove her upon this dangerous coast. In the midst of a blinding snow-storm, the unmanageable vessel was borne steadily and mercilessly upon the shore. When she struck, the shock brought down portions of her rigging, leaving her a dismantled wreck. As she began to sink, one by one the crew was picked off by the waves – only one reached the shore alive, fourteen died."*

Further down the beach at Race Point, a second light was erected in 1816, and on the seaward side of the Cape at Chatham and Nauset, four lighthouses once faced the always frothing ocean from high sand cliffs. Over the years, however, all these lighthouses faced annihilation from the receding sand, and either had to be abandoned or physically moved to avoid falling over the cliffs. The last to be moved was Cape Cod Light at Truro in June of 1996 after the Atlantic had eaten away at some 499 feet of sand dune since 1797, leaving it about to topple into the ocean. Even after these Cape Cod lighthouses displayed their guiding lights; there was on average, three serious shipwrecks off the Cape each year since their inception.

The only Cape Cod lighthouse not attached to the mainland is Cleveland Ledge Light, two miles from the southern entrance of the Cape Cod Canal. It sits on an underwater ledge surrounded by Shoal Waters. Erected in 1940, it is 52 feet high and 52 feet wide, built in one piece at New London, Connecticut, then towed and secured to the site. Its baptism came four years after its placement, when the September 1944 hurricane hit the area. Nine coastguard men were aboard her when waves smashed in the glass skylight and flooded the living and work chambers. All radio equipment was shorted out, but the men kept the lantern aglow by constant bailing and they were able to ride out the storm. Cleveland Ledge Light today probably sees more traffic than any other Atlantic lighthouse as vessel commanders opt for voyaging through the canal at the base of the Cape than cruising the rough seas of the outer Cape and around the Provincetown hook into the busy ports of Boston, Portsmouth and Portland, or sailing the opposite way to Newport or New York.

Probably the most horrific disaster of all time to inundate a reputed North Atlantic Graveyard came in 1938 to Southeastern Massachusetts and Rhode Island, conceivably ending all dispute as to the worst storm devastation and fury ever experienced in one seaside area. The aftermath of this unexpected North Atlantic hurricane, in my estimation, makes this one day occurrence the most treacherous incident on the high seas or along the coast that has ever confronted any graveyard of ships in North America or Europe. She struck Cape Hatteras on September 20th, then skipped along the ocean heading north, picking up steam as she covered 600 miles within twelve hours. Weather forecasters predicted she'd go out to sea, but with a new great surge of power, she smashed into Long Island, Connecticut, Rhode Island and Southeastern Massachusetts, including Cape Cod. This unnamed, unexpected hurricane eventually enveloped almost all of New England, but her 130 mile-an-hour winds and tidal waves concentrated on New Bedford, Rhode Island and the outer Elizabeth Islands. Construction supervisor Charles Cahoon was working near the Coast Guard Station at Cuttyhunk Island, one of the Elizabeth Chain, when, at mid afternoon on the 21st, the storm crept in from the sea. *"The Coast Guard Station's pet Airdale was sleeping in a little shack beside the Station,"* Cahoon later reported, *"when the storm broke, and the dog and shack were carried into the water by the first giant wave, and waves began dashing up forty feet on the lighthouse...The next morning, the dog came swimming in from the open sea practically exhausted, with nobody knowing how far out he had been swept."*

Looking out to sea from the golf course he managed at Marion, Massachusetts, Ray Dennehy saw *"at Bird Island Lighthouse, just offshore, there was a two story house I could see that was being smashed up. Water was at least two-thirds of the way up the lighthouse itself. Pretty soon I saw the wreckage of the building on Bird Island come floating by."* Before the day was out, 89 homes at Marrion would meet a similar fate. At Mattapoisett, 170 cottages were swept out to sea and at Sakonnet, 50 homes were wrecked. At Wareham, Massachusetts, often called the Gateway to Cape Cod, 325 homes were destroyed. When a great flood of water poured through the Cape Cod Canal, traveling at over 15-knots, houses along the embankment were torn loose and floated downstream. One home with four people inside floated many hundreds of yards until it crashed into the Bourne Bridge and sank, drowning three people inside. A New York to Boston train carrying 252 passengers, was stopped at Stonington, Connecticut because a 40-foot schooner had washed onto the trestle and the sea was covering the tracks. Soon, fishing trawlers and houses began smashing into the passenger cars, threatening to plunge them into the sea. Fast thinking railroad men had all the passengers wade to the front of the train as the flooding rear cars were uncoupled. Then the engineer smashed through all the debris to bring his passengers to dry land and safety, resulting in only two deaths by drowning. In the Rhode Island town of Westerly along an eight-mile stretch of coastal dwellings, only two of 169 residents remained alive. The seaside village of Narragansett was also wiped up by *"a tidal wave seventy feet high that came over the beach,"* reported one survivor. At Charleston, Rhode Island, 659 homes were destroyed by fierce winds and monstrous seas. In all, 4,500 homes were destroyed, 2,605 boats, with 3,370 damaged, 26,000 automobiles were ruined, 708 people were seriously injured and 680 lives were lost. Crops were destroyed, hundreds of thousands of trees were uprooted, as were most electric light and telephone poles, yet the storm didn't last for more than three hours. For coastal dwellers, it was over at nightfall. Inland, however, also got full brunt of it, especially Providence, Rhode Island, where over fifteen feet of water covered most city streets, and those city folks who couldn't swim, drowned. As the big waves roared up Narragansett Bay, they swallowed Whale Rock Lighthouse and the keeper's house, with Keeper Walter Eberley inside it. The Fisher Sound Latimer Reef Light was reduced to a pile of rocks, but Keeper George Durfee escaped, and the Lighthouse Tender Tulip was thrown ashore, high and dry at New London, Connecticut. At Rhode Island's Bullock Point Lighthouse, walls of water tore away the outside walls and stairs, but keeper Andrew Zuius kept the light burning even though his world was tumbling down around him.

At Jamestown, Rhode Island, off Newport, Keeper Carl Chellis at Beavertail Light tried to keep the lantern shining throughout the storm, but the pounding wind and waves extinguished the beacon and tore down the fog-whistle house. Unknown to Keeper Chellis however, was a tragedy unfolding only a few miles away. A school bus with eight elementary school children aboard was crossing a low causeway at Mackerel Cove, Jamestown, when the tidal wave hit. Bus driver Norman Caswell later exclaimed that, *"a huge sea struck us, and I saw that we would have to leave the bus or be drowned like rats. I told the children to grab each other tightly. I had hold of several when the huge wave came over us. I went down twice. When I came up I saw Clayton Chellis, the keeper's son swimming around. He was the only one who was saved besides me. He said that when I let them out of the bus, he was holding his little sister's hand; she was only seven, and the last thing he remembered was that she told him, 'Clayton, don't let the water get in your eyes.'"* She was the lighthouse keeper's daughter. *"When the lighthouse keeper arrived on the scene, he got mad,"* said a bystander, *"and he went down to the road and he took some rocks and he just crashed them windows out of that bus until he bust them all."* The bus driver was so despondent that he tried to drown himself after being rescued. *"Please let me die,"* he cried, *"I lost all those bunch of kids. Everything's gone. Please don't move me from the water. Let me die!"*

Close by on Prudence Island in Narragansett Bay, Keeper George Gustavus felt the storm coming in his bones and he secured the Light as best he could "before all hell broke loose." Also living on the sandy beach section of the island was a former keeper named Thompson, who immediately came to stay with Keeper Gustavus and his family at the lighthouse when the storm commenced. *"If anything remains standing on this island, it will be this house"* said Thompson, but giant waves broke through windows and doors, flooding every room and then finally collapsing the building. All five people who had sought shelter in the keeper's house, except Gustavus himself, were swept away and never seen again. The keeper was found in the midst of debris almost a mile from where the lighthouse stood and he was dragged ashore, battered and bruised, but still alive – his family, however, was gone.

At the same time, one of Gustavus' best friends, who he had entered the lighthouse service with some twenty-five years earlier, was in similar trouble on little Palmer Island in New Bedford Harbor. Keeper Arthur Small also anticipated the storm and boarded up all windows but the lighthouse lens. Like Gustavus, he could feel a good blow coming in his bones. He had previously been keeper at Bug Light in Boston Harbor. With him alone on the island that afternoon of September 21, 1938, was his wife Mabel. The storm hit with a force never before experienced by Keeper Small. Waves swept over the island, dragging everything into the sea. Small feared for the safety of his wife, but she refused to leave the keeper's quarters for the lighthouse tower, which was quivering as every wave struck. Finally, the house started crumbling around her, and dodging waves, she ran for the oil shed, where the lighthouse fuel was kept. Keeper Small, thinking Mabel was safe, tried to get to the fog bell, for he knew the Nantucket boat would be coming by the island with 200 women and children aboard. As he approached the bell, a forty-foot wave enveloped him and he was swept off the island. Mabel Small, witnessing this, tried to launch the lighthouse tender to save her husband, but as she did, another gigantic wave crashed into the boathouse, collapsing it with Mabel Small under it. Arthur actually witnessed his wife go underwater and never return to the surface. Barely conscious and badly bruised, Keeper Small managed to swim back to the island and crawl up the spiral stairs to the lighthouse lens room, where he was found the next day by two friends who rowed out from the mainland. Arthur Small was taken to a Boston hospital, and when completely revived, was amazed to find his old friend, Keeper George Gustavus in the bed next to his – both men had lost their wives to the hurricane. It had been an awesome force, which neither keeper had ever experienced before, nor wished to ever experience again. Both retired from lighthouse service after the 1938 Hurricane. It was the worst natural disaster in American history, and deemed this area the undisputed Graveyard of the North Atlantic, until a greater storm comes along someday.

Aftermath of the 1938 Hurricane: (R) Lighthouse tender TULIP is greeted by a train after being thrown onto the tracks at New London; Keeper Andrew Zuius surveys damage at Rhode Island's Bullock Point Light; and seven children drown in flooded bus, one being the lighthouse keeper's daughter.
Photos courtesy the Hartford Current.

Matinicus Rock Lighthouse, Maine, where 16- year old Abbie Burgess became a heroin.
U.S. Coast Guard photo.

Scuba diver Brad Luther (left) and Courtney Gifford of Fairhaven are set to dive on the Vineyard Sound Lightship, which disappeared for 19 years. (Lower) The Lightship's beacon light is raised to the surface by the divers.

The Diamond Shoals Lightship, snaps her anchor cables three times while stationed off Cape Hatteras. The third time she grounded at Oracoke Island and was sold for scrap. The Nantucket Lightship marked dangerous shoal waters for many years and is now a museum in Quincy, Massachusetts.

U.S. Coast Guard photos.

Chapter 8
For Whom the Bell Tolls

It took four difficult years to build the 75-foot high lighthouse at Eilean Mor, a cluster of rocks located some twenty miles off the Isle of Lewis in the Outer Hebrides. Eilean Mor is one of seven small islands or islets called Flannan Isles, or in ancient times, the Seven Hunters. Its cliffs rise some 200 feet out of a boiling sea, spanning an area of some 500 by 200 yards. Prior to 1899 when the lighthouse was completed, the only other building on the tiny island was the ruin of a church built by Saint Flannan in the 1600s. Since it was almost impossible to land on Eilean Mor when the sea was up, landing platforms with stairways etched in the rocks leading to a lighthouse were constructed and winches were installed to lift men and supplies from lighthouse tenders when they weren't able to land on the island. The tenders were sturdy vessels built specifically by the governments to set navigational buoys and service lightships and lighthouses. The tender for the Eilean Mor Lighthouse was the steamship HESPERUS, which would visit with needed supplies and relief workers every two weeks. Other than the lighthouse personnel and the HESPERUS captain and crew, no one else visited the lonely island of Eilean Mor. This was the belief until probably the greatest lighthouse mystery of all time unfolded there the day after Christmas in the year 1900.

Of the four who tended the lighthouse, Joseph Moore, Donald McArthur, James Ducat and Tom Marshall, Moore had been on leave since December 6th. Moore should have returned earlier to relieve McArthur, but severe weather delayed the HESPERUS visit to the island until the 26th. The keepers had gone without holiday food as well as Christmas mail and packages, and McArthur had missed being at home with his family. Returning to work aboard the HESPERUS, Joseph Moore was worried that his colleagues were probably in a bad mood. He was further troubled by the reports from the passing vessels that said that the light from the Eilean Mor Lighthouse hadn't shone for the last few nights. Moore concluded that the mariners who reported this blackout were wrong. He was sure that foul and foggy weather had caused them to miss the light, which was usually visible for some forty miles. Surely the three light keepers, no matter how severe the weather or the situation, would never allow the light to go out.

Before attempting to land at the island platform, the HESPERUS skipper gave a few powerful blasts on his fog whistle to let the keepers know he had arrived. He flew the signal flag which indicated the relief keeper, Joe Moore, was aboard and that McArthur should get himself and his dufflebag to the platform to be hoisted aboard so that he could take a two week leave. No one arrived at the platform and there was no sign of life from the lighthouse. Instead of making an attempt to land the HESPERUS, the skipper had two of his men row Joe Moore to the platform in a longboat. Moore had the boatmen wait on the platform while he climbed to the lighthouse. The door to the structure was closed, but unlocked. Inside he called for his fellow workers but there was no answer. Moore nervously walked from compartment to compartment within the lighthouse as the HESPERUS bobbed on the giant swells outside the rocks below. Everything seemed in order, but the living quarters' clock had stopped and the fire in the kitchen stove had gone out. The daytime cloth covering of the light lens was not in place, which was against regulations. Nothing else seemed to be out of place. The lantern wicks were trimmed, the machinery had been cleaned and the quarters were clean and neat. The last entry in the lighthouse log was the morning of December 15th, but it gave no indication of extreme weather or anything else unusual. Moore was suddenly frozen with fear, not only because of his missing friends, but because the HESPERUS skipper might decide to leave the island, thinking Moore was safe and sound aboard the lighthouse. He signaled the HESPERUS skipper that he needed help.

The HESPERUS sent a second longboat ashore and the crew started combing the rocky treeless island for the missing men or for any clue they might find to explain what might have happened to them. After a thorough investigation of the island and the lighthouse by Moore and the HESPERUS crew, the only odd findings were that the iron railing along the cliff stairway was broken in places, which could have been caused by a giant freak wave. Ducat and Marshall's raingear and boots were missing from their lockers. Could they have been down on the landing and carried off by a monstrous wave? If so, what became of McArthur, whose foul weather gear was still in his locker? Two of the HESPERUS crew were reluctantly left behind on Eilean Mor with Joe Moore. He lit the lighthouse lamp as the HESPERUS returned to the mainland for help. Police and military personal were there swarming the next day. They were there for months after the HESPERUS skipper reported the mystery to authorities, but no trace of the whereabouts of the three lighthouse keepers was ever found. Their disappearance still remains a mystery.

Exactly sixty years later, the lighthouse-tender HESPERUS was involved in another lighthouse mystery, off the coast of Isle of Man at a reef lighthouse called Chickens Rock. Unlike Eilean Mor, the 85 year old Chickens Rock Lighthouse, towering 150-feet above the waves, was completely surrounded by water at high tide. Therefore the three keepers could not leave the tower but at low or ebb tides. On the morning of December 23, 1960, while the three keepers were in the upper chambers of the lighthouse there was an explosion, and flames came shooting up into the tower. It was never established what caused the explosion, but fire and smoke drove the keepers up into the lens room and then onto the narrow iron balcony that encompassed the light. There seemed no escape and the men believed they would be burned alive. Tying off manila lines, one to the other, they discovered that they had just enough rope to reach the rocks below. Since the tide was receding, they could slide down safely, which they did one at a time. The last keeper down, however, was severely burned about the legs as he made his descent. As the lighthouse burned down around them, the men huddled as close to the base as possible. They did this for warmth, but the tide was soon coming in and could drown them in the icy waves. It seemed that at one minute they would die of one extreme, and the next minute, from another. A gale wind was now blowing, which fanned the flames and started to make it hotter than desired on the slippery rocks. There were also fuel storage tanks in the upper chamber and once the fire reached them, a second explosion could be of such magnitude it would probably blow them into the sea, or to kingdom come.

Luckily a passing freighter had spotted the smoking lighthouse and informed the British Admirality, who in turn, dispatched the Navy lifeboat COLBY CUBBIN. She arrived on the scene just after noon, but the heavy seas and flames wouldn't allow the CUBBIN and her crew to come closer than a few hundred feet of the island reef. Over a loudspeaker, the skipper of the CUBBIN ordered the keepers to tie a line to the base of the lighthouse, with a stick secured to the other end of the line, which they would allow to float out to the tender. The CUBBIN now had a line to the lighthouse, over which they passed a breeches-buoy to the keepers. The keepers then strapped the badly burned keeper into the buoy. The CUBBIN crew started hauling him to the tender, but a massive wave smashed into the breeches-buoy, capsizing it and dumping the injured keeper into the frothing high seas. Half drowned, he managed to reach the CUBBIN with the help of the crew and was pulled to safety. Meanwhile, the storm had forced an early high tide and the two remaining keepers on the reef were clinging to the lighthouse-landing platform. Here they were covered with icy spray at every wave. With the breeches-buoy broken, there seemed no way to help the two struggling men. The CUBBIN skipper called for a rescue helicopter, and within minutes one was hovering over the burning lighthouse. There was no way the helicopter men could rescue the keepers without burning up the aircraft, and they regrettably left the scene. Two new rescue boats arrived, the Port Erin lifeboat MATTHEW SIMPSON and the old lighthouse tender HESPERUS. It was now high tide and neither could approach the reef without putting the vessel and crew in jeopardy. They all watched helplessly as the two keepers, frozen to numbness and seared with burns, were tossed and slammed against the rocks and concrete slab by giant waves that lashed the sizzling lighthouse. In a miraculous spirit of survival, the two held on until the tide turned, once again exposing the surrounding rocks. Their clothes had been torn away by the actions of the waves and they shivered uncontrollably from the cold, but they had lasted eight hours through intolerable heat, flames, cold, wet and constant battering. The crew of the CUBBIN could look on no more and they pleaded with their skipper to maneuver in for a daring rescue. As the CUBBIN made a cautious approach, the crew reached over the rail, tore the keepers from their frigid perch and hauled them aboard. They were alive, but barely. The rescuers headed for port with their survivors as the HESPERUS remained on station until the lighthouse fire extinguished itself. The HESPERUS then placed a flashing beacon at the scene to replace the 85-year old light that had never before failed. The rock skeleton of the Chickens Rock Lighthouse remains to this day, off the Isle of Man, but her faithful light never shined again. The cause of the explosion and fire was never determined. The lighthouse tender HESPERUS, however, bore witness once again to one of the greatest lighthouse mysteries of the North Atlantic.

Lighthouse tenders like the HESPERUS were an integral part of the lighthouse service in Britain and America from the early 1800s through the 1950s. Each nation supported approximately fifty such vessels at one time to service remote offshore lighthouses, and to set and maintain buoys and other navigational aids. They were also a necessary link with the mainland for lightboats, later called lightships, which were anchored securely off treacherous reefs instead of permanent lighthouses. It was argued as early as 1730 that lightboats were more beneficial to mariners than lighthouses, especially at dangerous shoals along the coasts. This was mainly because they were cheaper to build and maintain and they offered beacons in sandy areas where land was eroding and might topple a lighthouse. Sailors could sail right up to a lightboat to get accurate compass bearings. The lightboat also carried a fogbell that was easier heard from a floating sentinel than somewhere on shore. Although the Romans prior to the birth of Christ had used vessels carrying torches to guide ships into harbors and around reefs, the first official lightboat of the North Atlantic was a single-masted sloop. This had two lanterns suspended ten feet apart on a mast cross-arm and was anchored permanently at Nore Sandbank, at the mouth of the Thames River, England in 1731. In America, the first lightboat was placed on station at Willoughby Spit, Virginia in 1820. The first open-ocean lightship, located off the U.S. coast, was at Sandy Hook, New Jersey in 1823. It remained on station for 83 years.

The Diamond Shoals Lightship took station thirteen miles east of Cape Hatteras in June of 1824, but it remained only eight months when a February storm ripped the vessel from its great anchor and did heavy damage to the lightship before her skipper managed to bring her into Norfolk. There, it took almost a year to repair her damages. She returned to station in December 1825, only to have her anchor chain snap again five months later. Captain Lief was forced to bring her in once more to Norfolk, Virginia. Resuming her post in November 1826, she lasted nine months before her mooring cable snapped again and wild winds drove the Diamond Shoals Lightship onto Ocracoke

Island. She remained here in the sand until broken up for salvage and drift-wood.

Better luck was had with lightboats stationed off Nantucket Island, Massachusetts. Nine separate vessels were moored near and around the island as navigational aids by 1873. Much of the shoal waters surrounding Nantucket were too treacherous to build lighthouses. It was decided that large seaworthy vessels anchored in or close to the shoal waters, carrying a tower of light like a lighthouse, and a large clanging bell, would serve the many mariners and fishermen who cruised the waters. Nantucket Shoals, some forty miles from the nearest land is almost directly in the path of the most traveled sea lane in the world, the entrance to New York Harbor from Europe. This storm tossed, fog plagued shoal area was, *"in desperate need of a beacon and a bell."* A Congressional report of 1843 reads that *"there is still another more fatal spot than Minots Ledge upon the coast of Massachusetts, where man of brave heart and many a gallant ship lie buried in one common grave. The shoals of Nantucket are known and dreaded by every navigator on the Atlantic seaboard; and among the great number of missing vessels."*

The first lightship placed on duty off Nantucket was an old converted whaling ship called the Tuckernuck Shoals Lightship. It remained, crewed by four old retired whalers, from 1828 to 1848. Tuckernuck Shoals is what is known today as Cross Rip, where the warm Gulf Stream meets the Arctic Current, keeping the water there at a constant boil. The lightship often dragged anchor or parted her cables and drifted off her station during her twenty years of service. The old salts merely lifted her sails and maneuvered her back to the station; however, this sometimes took days to do so. In 1849, the PRESIDENT, a newer whaling ship, replaced her. The PRESIDENT was considered more seaworthy, but she wasn't. The whaler parted her anchor after four years on station, swamped, and was damaged beyond repair.

The first Nantucket Shoals Lightship, located nineteen miles off the island, was anchored on site in 1854, but she broke her cable within a year on station and drifted onto Montauk Point, Long Island. She was salvaged and repaired, but New York claimed her and stationed her offshore at Scotland Shoal, where she remained on duty for 65 years. The government built a new, sturdier lightship for Nantucket Shoals, and at about the same time, a more seaworthy and better-equipped vessel for Cross Rip as well. The Nantucket Shoals ship was 100 feet long with a rounded bottom and high bow to better ride the waves. Although, permanently moored offshore, she carried sails for power in the event her cables parted, which happened more than once. Yet, she served successfully for over 36 years, from 1856 to 1892. She was then towed to Savannah, Georgia, serving as the Martins Industry Lightship. She was given the new name, "Light Vessel Number One." The vessel that replaced her at

Nantucket Shoals was moved permanently forty miles off the island, twice as far out to sea as the lightships before her.

A specially built, supposedly sturdier, Cross Rip Lightship to replace the whaling ship PRESIDENT was on a heavy mushroom mooring in 1859. Then, a furious gale ripped her from that mooring five years later and she drifted onto Cape Poge, Martha's Vineyard. She was smashed to pieces and was completely destroyed, but the lightship crew did manage to scramble safely ashore. There was a question on whether or not the Cross-Rip Lightship should be replaced, for many skippers who accidentally drove their vessels ashore on Great Point Rip blamed the Cross-Rip Lightship for wrecking their vessels. On April 17, 1864, Captain Stephen Jones of the schooner WILLIAM JONES reported that he mistook the lightship light for Great Point Lighthouse, and instead of sailing into Nantucket, he wrecked his schooner on the sandy reef. Two other vessels made the same mistake that same year, and another hit the bar in October of the following year, her skipper also complaining that he thought the light of the lightship was the lighthouse. The schooner LEESBURG of Maine also smashed into Great Point Rip the following September, and again it was a case of mistaken identity. The lighthouse keeper never reported these complaints to his supervisors in Washington D.C., for fear the Great Point Lighthouse would be closed down. The accidents continued on for years without a solution. The keeper also feared that locals might burn down the light as they had in 1816, supposedly because it interfered with wrecking activities in this lonely area. When Samuel Smith, Commissioner of the U.S. Revenue Department investigated the fire that gutted the stone tower, he reported that, *There is no doubt that the Lighthouse was purposely set on fire, but who did it could never be proved.*

A new Cross Rip Lightship was built by the government and placed back on station in October 1865, under command of Ben Gardner. This was the first to be painted bright red, with great white letters on both port and starboard sides reading: "CROSS RIP." Fourteen months later, on the day after Christmas, 1866, the Cross-Rip Lightship disappeared in a blizzard. Captain Gardner however, hadn't been aboard her. He was in Nantucket celebrating Christmas with his family. Search teams were sent out in an effort to find the lightship and her crew but to no avail. Every nearby port was contacted in hopes that the lightship might have sailed in after slipping her mooring, but no one along the East Coast had seen the Cross Rip Lightship. Her brightly colored sides and large lettering would have made her easily recognizable. Mariners, however, swore that they heard the lightship's fogbell ringing for days after Christmas, even though the lightship was not there. Not one body or a single piece of wreckage from the lightship washed ashore. After a month without a clue as to how or why the ship and men disappeared, memorial services were held for the crew at Nantucket. However, the grieving families of the crewmen were revived on the morning of January 31, 1867, when a message arrived at the Nantucket tele-graph office from New Orleans, Louisiana. It was from the crew of the Cross-Rip Lighthouse, they were alive. First mate Charles Thomas explained that in the hurricane force winds, the anchor cables snapped and the vessel drifted off with waves so large and powerful that their lifeboat was stove in and the main-sail was torn to shreds. Then water filled the compartments and slowly flooded every cabin. The crew was exhausted from bailing, pumping and trying to keep the lightship afloat for four days. They were constantly at the mercy of the wind and waves until finally the men were resigned to their fate, when the ship H.L. RICHARDSON of Maine spotted them in distress. The RICHARDSON captain sent a boat, into which all crewmen escaped the lightship, only moments before she went under. The RICHARDSON was heading for New Orleans, and thus, that's where the lucky crew of the Cross-Rip Lightship ended up. When they returned to Nantucket weeks later, they were given a heroes welcome; but government authorities weren't too pleased with loosing two Cross Rip Lightships within two years.

Replacements at Cross Rip served successfully for fifty years without any major dilemmas, but on February 5, 1918, the keeper of the Great Point Lighthouse witnessed a strange phenomenon. He saw the Cross-Rip Lightship being pulled from her cable and forced slowly but surely out to sea by large masses of ice. The lightship and her six-man crew disappeared – swept out to sea in an ice field. Only one item in the Nantucket newspaper provided any insight as to what might have destroyed her: *"Whether the lightship passed over the rips and shoals and went out into the deep sea is a matter for conjec-ture. If she struck on the Rose and Crown Shoals, or Bass Rip, or some other shoal, there is small chance that any of her men escaped, as the powerful ice would soon make quick work of a small craft like that. On the afternoon of the disappearance of the lightship, the keepers at Sankaty reported what looked like a bellbuoy encased in ice showing up about four miles east south-east from the Round Shoals Lightship. That object may have been the tower of the Cross Rip Vessel."* There was no other clue of the disappearance until 39 years later, when in April of 1957, beach-comber Robert Crowell of Dennis on Cape Cod uncovered a Waterbury clock from deep under the sandy beach at Dennis. The clock was identified as being aboard the lightship when she was carried off in the ice. Also uncovered at the beach was a five-foot sideboard with the name *"CROSS RIP"* carved into it.

There have been many other incidents of lightships being carried off by ice-flows. In 1875, seven Massachusetts lightships were swept from their stations by ice, but all managed to break free and return to their moorings. A lightship, of course, was not allowed to leave her station for any reason, and to be dragged off position could mean disaster for passing ships that relied on her light and bell to be in a fixed position. Many lightships, however, were constructed without masts and rigging for sailing and had no means of power, which made it impossible for them to return to station when forced off by wind, wave or ice, unless assisted by a lighthouse tender or other large vessel. In a November gale of 1898, the Pollock Rip Lightship was driven some 300 miles out of Massachusetts waters to Delaware, mainly because her crew had no means to stop her from drifting. When she arrived in Delaware, the authorities there thought at first that she was a federal government gift, for only five years earlier, their own lightship at Five-Fathom Bank had floundered and sank at her mooring. In the 150-year history of lightships in the North Atlantic, hardly more than two or three foundered while at anchor on station. Besides the Five-Fathom Bank Lightship, the Nantucket Shoals Lightship also suffered this embarrassment in 1905. But, it was her Relief Lightship and not the Nantucket Lightship herself that sprung a leak and had to call the lighthouse tender AZALEA for assistance. The AZALEA attempted to tow her into New Bedford before she filled and went under, but before reaching port, the crew abandoned ship, the towline was cut and the lightship sank. In addition, three British lightships were torpedoed by German U-boats or bombarded by airplanes while on station during the World Wars, but the Germans destroyed only one American lightship of the North Atlantic while on her mooring. The Diamond Shoals Lightship was attacked on August 6, 1918. A German U-boat commander, after allowing the twelve men of the crew to abandon ship, sank the lightship with the submarine's deckgun.

Although snapping a cable while riding out a storm was a major concern for lightship sailors, collision with another vessel was probably their greatest fear. In many instances, they were anchored in the middle of shipping channels that were often fogged in, making them a stationary target to any vessel off a few degrees on the compass. Boston Lightship with a bright red hull and "Boston" in big white letters decorating her sides, was rammed twice in 1894 by vessels off course coming into Boston Harbor. Cross Rip experienced collisions with fifteen barges and seven schooners from 1886 to 1894. The first lightship to house electric light at Cornfield Point, Connecticut, was also the first in New England to be sunk by a barge at her mooring in April 1919. New York's Fire Island Lightship, established in 1896, was collided with twice in 1915 and 1916, the later sealing her fate. The British steamer EASTERN CITY slammed into her head on and she immediately started to fill with water. Listing badly, she was towed into New York City, but was never returned to duty at Fire Island. She was replaced by a stationary, thirty-foot whistling buoy. The 12,000-ton Swedish liner STOCKHOLM that collided with and sank the Italian liner ANDREA DORIA on July 25, 1956, also smashed into and heavily damaged the Hens and Chickens Lightship off Cape Cod. The lightship Gull was severely damaged off the West Coast of England in a fog, when rammed by the steamer CITY OF YORK in 1929. Thus, by attrition and collision, the lightship service was all but concluded by the 1970's. There were only three lightships still serving the American East Coast in 1973. All lightships had been replaced by unmanned, lighted whistling- buoys. Only one, the Nantucket Lightship remains on duty today, still displaying her light every night. She is currently snug and protected in North Quincy Bay, Massachusetts, a floating museum.

At Nauset Lifesaving Museum at the Cape Cod National Seashores, the remnants of one old lightship remains on display, and her old fogbell periodically moans and echoes over the sand dunes. It is an eerie, ghostly sound, and it is a reminder of the bell's strange fate, and the tragedy that befell the men who once rang her in the dense fog that often blankets Vineyard Sound. The bell was specifically built for the 112-foot Vineyard Sound Lightship, stationed permanently off Cuttyhunk Island near the entrance to Buzzards Bay and the Cape Cod Canal. Twelve Coast Guardsmen remained on duty at all times aboard the lightship, keeping her light ablaze at night. Sometimes they had to ring the bell manually for a constant twenty-four hours as fog or sea mist blinded skippers and navigators tried to find a safe passage around the many reefs that speckle the area. It was on the evening of September 14, 1944, that the wind began to shriek like a banshee. The sea lifted the lightship in great swells, and the bell, firmly attached to the forward deck, began to toll on its own. It tolled the final hours of the Vineyard Sound Lightship and her crew. When the storm that lashed the Cape for six hours subsided, there was little damage ashore, but the lightship was missing from her mooring. Months passed and she could not be found. Then years passed, and except for family and friends of the crew, she was forgotten. She became an unsolved mystery; the ship and all aboard her vanished without a trace.

Brad Luther, a fireman from Fairhaven, Massachusetts, was only a boy when the Vineyard Sound Lightship disappeared, but the mystery plagued him. As he grew older, he resolved himself to solve it. Scuba diving was a new sport and past time in the late 1950's, and Brad was one of its pioneers. He organized a diving club in his hometown, the "Fairhaven Whalers," with its main purpose to find the Vineyard Lightship. Brad had concluded she was still somewhere in Buzzards Bay. Reading of Brad's efforts in the Boston newspapers, noted M.I.T. inventor Harold Edgerton contacted him. Edgerton was testing a new side-scan sonar device he had invented, and was willing to bring it to Buzzards Bay to help Brad and his diving club. Edgerton's scanner could chart the ocean bottom, providing a side angle profile sketch of any unusual object in the bay. The inventor and the diver joined forces. After Brad and his team had spent some six years scouring the bay underwater in search of the lightship, on September 2, 1963, Edgerton's side-scan sonar recorded a large object underwater at a depth of seventy feet, nine miles off the coast of Westport, Massachusetts. Diving down through murky water, Brad came face to face with a mass of twisted metal imbedded in sand and weed. In the midst of this rubble was a giant bell. He was on the wreck of the Vineyard Sound Lightship – missing for nineteen years.

On the anniversary of her sinking, Luther, with his team of divers, descended on the wreck with the intent of salvaging items for posterity. They found the bow and after-decks still intact at seventy feet. The mushroom anchor setting upright on the sandy floor, was close to a deep gash in the ship's bow. This led Luther to theorize that the mushroom anchor, which usually hangs over the rail of the ship to be used in emergencies, might have broken loose during the storm. With the anchor swinging and crashing into bow plates, water could have flooded into the lightship and caused her to sink. Brad noted that the hole in the bow was located in the chain locker, a place where the coast guardsmen couldn't reach to stop the intake of water. The divers attached a cable from their surface boat, the ninety-foot SYLVIA MAE, to the sunken fogbell. Other smaller articles were brought to the surface by Luther's team of scuba divers: the lightship's binnacle and compass, donated to the M.I.T. Museum; a Springfield rifle, a sextant, dishes, cups and the ship's brass clock. Brad Luther personally brought the clock to the surface, but half way up the clock exploded in his arms. *"I wasn't injured,"* reported Luther, *"but I was startled. Apparently water had seeped into the mechanism, compressing the air inside it. The air expanded as I carried the clock into a lighter atmosphere, which in turn, caused the explosion."*

What startled Brad more than the clock explosion was the rough seas he encountered when he reached the surface. A squall had set in which the divers couldn't feel below, and the SYLVIA MAE had snapped her anchor cable. The only lines holding her on site was the line tied to the bell on the bottom, and another knotted to the Vineyard Sound's beacon light, which they also hoped to salvage. With the weather closing in on them, Brad called all of his divers to the surface. The line to the beacon was reluctantly cut, for Brad felt they could attempt to salvage only the bell in such high seas, and even that proved to be a dangerous chore. With winches whirling, the SYLVIA MAE heeled over and the cable went taut. There was a snap and the line wound freely on the drum. The bell had broken from the wreckage. With the dive boat in precarious seas, the bell broke to the surface, rusty and covered with sea moss. The boys sent up a cheer, the boat engine was started and they cruised into New Bedford Harbor with the fogbell lashed to the stern of the dive boat. Many gathered at the old whaling dock, as the bell was unloaded to dry land. It echoed a chilling *"clang, clang, clang,"* twelve times, as it was lifted to the dock, as if to remind all present of the twelve who drowned aboard the Vineyard Sound Lightship. The bell, now cleaned and polished is permanently mounted at Nauset, as a memorial to the lighthouse tender crewmen and the lightship sailors who pledged themselves to protect the lives and property of other mariners. It is for these courageous men that the bell now tolls.

Chapter 9
Shadows On The Spiral Stairs

The lonely life of a lighthouse keeper, marooned on some desolate island or foreboding reef, lends itself perfectly to tales of ghosts, demons and things that go bump in the night. Almost every lighthouse in the North Atlantic, once, manned by courageous keepers and now automated, has a spooky story or chilling legend attached to it. Many have faded or dissipated with time. Almost from the day lighthouses were first erected along the coast, keepers were reporting strange sightings. As early as 1786 the Cows Head Lighthouse Keeper in Northumberland Strait, Canada, swore to authorities that he saw from his perch in the tower, *"a three-masted schooner under full sail in a nor'east gale, drive herself onto the cliffs below the light."* Then a rain squall blurred his vision, *"and when the rain subsided, the schooner had disappeared."* Since then, this same distressed schooner has been seen time and time again, well into the 1990s, along Prince Edward Island and the New Brunswick coast. Folks there have long ago concluded that the ill-fated schooner, seen first by the Cows Head Lighthouse Keeper, is a ghost ship, a phantom that prowls the coast, reenacting her demise over and over again through the centuries.

Further down the Canadian coast another phantom ship is seen periodically off Bon Portage Lighthouse, nine miles from Cape Sable Island, Nova Scotia. She is the schooner BELLE, built in 1860 at Lunenburg but owned in common by the people of the village of Shag Harbor, not far from Bon Portage Island. Villagers watched her coming in loaded with cargo on October 17, 1869. She had been away to Boston for many weeks. They could see their husbands, brothers and sons, passengers and crew aboard the BELLE as she slipped past Bon Portage and headed into Shag Harbor, but then there came a sudden snow squall. It ended as abruptly as it came, but when it did subside, the BELLE was nowhere in sight. She was never seen again, except in phantom form, and not a splinter of wood, nor a body from her decks ever washed ashore. Elizabeth Richardson, wife of the lighthouse keeper, writes that, her Uncle Gilbert, who witnessed the BELLE being swallowed up in the snow-squall, later reported that, *"my father and mother were standing out on their back steps, when they saw a schooner outside Bon Portage. She was clear and well defined against the sky-line. They turned their gaze away for a minute or two and then turned to look again at the schooner, but she was not there. They looked to see if their eyes had deceived them, but there was no schooner there, and it was impossible for her to sail out of sight in so short a time. They concluded it was a phantom vessel, to show the BELLE would never enter her home port again. "*

Bon Portage Lighthouse was notorious on the mainland as a haunted lighthouse. The first keeper, Michael Wrayton and his son Arthur, ran the lonely outpost until the Richardsons came in the 1920s. Arthur Wrayton's wife had been accused of murder, and that is what stimulated the ghost legend. Arthur's assistant keeper was a demented boy named *"Billy"*, and one day when Arthur was on the mainland, Billy was caught in a snow-squall, rowing close to the lighthouse. Billy cried for help, but Mrs. Wrayton, inside the lighthouse, refused to leave her young children alone in the tower to help Billy. Billy drowned and Mrs. Wrayton was accused of killing him. She, however, was found guilty of only negligence in not coming to his aid, but the court experience and accusations devastated her. To add to her troubles, her husband drowned at the lighthouse only a few weeks after her trial. Mrs. Wrayton moved to her childhood home in Halifax and died two years later. The ghosts of Billy, Arthur and his wife have all been seen time and again at the lighthouse by fishermen and mainlanders. Thus, when Elizabeth and Morrill Richardson took over the light, they found it difficult to get help from the mainland. *"One day, "* writes Mrs. Richardson, *"Morrill and I went to Shag Harbor to vote and took the children with us. The boat that came to take us off left two boys of about twelve to keep the Light, for although we left in the middle of the day and expected to be back in an hour or so, we were not supposed to leave the lighthouse unattended. As I left for the shore, I called to the lads that I had prepared a lunch for them, and told them where to find it. While we were away, the wind freshened from he south-west...and when we returned, the two boys were at the waters edge waiting to leave, and lost no time in getting away. At the house I found the lunch untouched, most unusual I thought... Years later, one of these lads, now a tall young man, came over to the island to help me, and I learnt why my lunch had gone uneaten. A south-west wind blows into our back porch, even when the outer door is closed, so strongly and in such a way that it opens the back door to the kitchen, which is fastened merely by a latch that drops into a slot and fits non too snugly. The two youngsters had spent a terror-stricken afternoon closing that back door and watching it open each time to reveal a complete absence of any human opener – they had been too scared to eat anything."* Fifteen years keeping the lighthouse at Bon Portage, and neither of the Richardsons saw the ghost. Mainlanders called the spirit, *"Wrayton's Ghost, "* but the Richardson children saw and played with *"Wrayton's Goat, "* and often blamed it for stealing cookies.

Further down the coast at the mouth of Maine's Saco River, another murder has prompted the sightings of a ghost at a lighthouse. It all began on June 1, 1896, when Sheriff Fred Milliken, who was also a local lobsterman of Biddleford Pool, reluctantly rented his chicken coop to an Old Orchard Beach bum named Howard Hobbs. Shortly thereafter, Hobbs, who drank too much rum, had an argument with Milliken's wife. Confronted by the armed Sheriff Milliken, who threatened to arrest him, Hobbs drew a weapon of his own. When the sheriff tried to confiscate the weapon, Hobbs shot him. Onlookers carried the fatally wounded Milliken into his house, with the help of Hobbs, but Hobbs insisted on holding onto his gun, which had one bullet left in the chamber. *"It is for me,"* said Hobbs, *"if Milliken dies."* Within twenty minutes Milliken was dead. Hobbs raced from the house, and for some unknown reason, ran to Keeper Orcutts home at the Wood Island Lighthouse. Orcutt pleaded with Hobbs to give up the gun, but he would not, *"and ten minutes later there was an explosion,"* Keeper Orcutt reported. Some believe it's the bulky giant Sheriff Milliken that now haunts the lighthouse, but most say it is the drifter Hobbs that is heard moaning from the direction of the old hen-house where he lived. Locked doors in the lighthouse have been found mysteriously opened by subsequent keepers. The keeper who replaced Orcutt, reported that he heard strange voices and saw dark shadows in the lantern room. He finally rowed ashore and rented a room in a boarding house, leaving the lighthouse lamp unlit that evening. The next morning, he jumped out of the third-story window of the boardinghouse, seemingly another victim of the harassing drifter Howard Hobbs.

The Wood Island Lighthouse lantern was removed in 1972, some say because the ghost was raising havoc with the light. Locals however, complained about their *"headless lighthouse,"* and so the Coast Guard replaced the lamp. Wood Island Light remains an active navigational aid, automated in 1986, but supposedly still watched over by the angry spirit of Howard Hobbs.

Another murder-suicide resulting in a resident lighthouse ghost, occurred at Sequin Island Light Station located two miles south of the mouth of Maine's Kennebec River. Besides whimsical spirits, this area is almost always fogged in with sea mist. The Sequin foghorn or *"steam-whistle"* of the early 20th century was louder than any in existence. It could be heard fifteen to twenty miles away, and said Keeper Frank Bracey in 1931, *"I saw seagulls knocked out of the sky by the concussion of the horn."* The name Sequin is from the Indian word *"Sutquin,"* which means *"sea vomit."* Besides the fog and wild waters surrounding the lighthouse, it's located one quarter mile up the steep side of a cliff, and from 1795 to the mid 1800s, supplies were back-packed up to the lighthouse from supply boats. It was such an isolated spot that in 1846 the keeper's wife threatened to leave him unless he could provide her with something to stem her boredom. Knowing she loved music, he shipped a piano to the island and had it winched up to the lighthouse. For awhile, the new piano seemed to fill the void for his wife, and she learned to play it on her own. However, she only learned one song, a ditty from her childhood days. She continued to play it over and over again, until she drove her poor husband stark raving mad. On the day the keeper could stand the music no longer, he took an ax and smashed the piano into firewood, and when his wife adamantly protested, he took the ax to her, and all but cut off her head. Then he killed himself. Even today, however, the old school ditty can still be heard on foggy nights, drifting down the Kennebec from inside the lighthouse.

A tramway was built from the water, 1.000 feet up with tracks and diesel powered car in the 1900s, to facilitate hauling supplies and getting people to and from Sequin Light. One day in 1949, when Keeper Irvine's wife and 18-month old daughter were riding in it, the car broke loose and tumbled down the cliff. The quick thinking Joyce Irvine tossed the baby on the grass without injuring her as she plummeted down the hill. It was the work, thought many locals, of the piano-playing ghost, who was angry and jealous that she didn't have such a fancy device to haul her and her goods up and down the cliff when she lived there. When Coast Guard personnel operated the light in the 1950s through 1985, before the light was automated, they had many ghostly encounters. Boatswain Mate Ed Brown reported that when the men were ready to leave the light for good in 1985, they were woken up the night before departure by an old salty looking character wearing wet oilskins. *"Don't take my furniture,"* he shouted at the warrant officer in charge, waking him from a sound sleep. *"Leave my house alone, "* he said. The warrant officer leaped out of bed and ran from the lighthouse. *"Obviously, "* says Brown, *"he wishes to remain anonymous, but he swears the ghost woke him up and made those demands of him."* Others had seen the old keeper around the lighthouse in his oilskins, tidying up here and there, always intent on chores, and never confronting anyone until he approached the warrant officer. The Coast Guardsmen departed on schedule the next day leaving the ghostly keeper and his piano playing wife behind at the automated Sequin Light.

The poor addicted keeper's wife of Bird Island Light off the coast of Marion, Massachusetts, suffered the same fate as the piano playing keeper's wife at Sequin. She was, it was thought, murdered by her husband. Her old ex-pirate husband said that she died from nicotine poisoning, but the mainlanders didn't believe him. The flamboyant Billy Moore came to little Bird Island as keeper, with his frail, quiet wife in 1815. She loved her pipe, but Billy wouldn't allow her to smoke because, he said, *"she has a consumptive cough."* Friends from Marion used to row out to her with tobacco when Billy was busy elsewhere. These visitors noted that the wife often displayed a black eye or a swollen jaw. It was obvious Billy was beating her, probably because he caught her smoking, but she either couldn't or wouldn't give up the pipe. One February morning, in 1832, the distress flag was flying from the lighthouse. There they found the bruised body of Mrs. Moore. Billy insisted on a quick burial, for he convinced the men that she had contagious tuberculosis and had succumbed to nicotine. A shallow grave was dug in the frozen earth of the little island. Rumor that she was murdered spread quickly at Marion, then called Sippican, until it came to the ear of the accused himself. Being an old pirate and master of deceit, Billy turned the guilt back on the villagers in a letter sent to the local authorities, he wrote: *"I found a bag containing tobacco among the clothes of my wife after her decease. It was furnished by certain individuals in and about Sippican. May the curses of High Heaven rest upon the heads of those who destroyed the peace of my family and the health of my wife."* The letter, however, didn't stop the rumors and only made the local sheriff that much more suspicious. When the sheriff decided to investigate further, it was too late, Keeper Moore had disappeared, leaving the lighthouse without a keeper, and his wife's grave without a headstone. Another keeper was appointed and came to Bird Island with his family, but they soon left the island in fright, telling stories of seeing the ghost of an old woman who kept coming knocking to the lighthouse door at night. She had her hand held out in front of her as if begging for something – tobacco no doubt. A second and third keeper were hired, but all refused to stay on the island for any length of time, and the keeper's house was torn down in 1890, for lack of willing occupants. The ghost of the worn, stoop-shouldered Mrs. Moore is still seen from time to time on Bird Island. Once in 1982, when the harbor was frozen over, like on the day she died, two local fishermen, Chuck Gordon and Adam Larkin, reported seeing the misty figure of a *"disfigured and tattered looking old woman crossing the ice from Bird Island, an old corn cob pipe clenched in her jaw. She seemed to float over the ice, hell bent for the mainland,"* – off searching for her bag of tobacco, no doubt.

There is also another haunted Bird Island, with both male and female spirits frequenting the lighthouse, at Canada's Magdalen Island group off Cape Breton. It is here that islands and lighthouses are iced in during the winter months, and great herds of seals live on the icepacks in the Gulf of Saint Lawrence. Lighthouse keepers become seal hunters and supplement their low pay by killing seals and selling seal skins. This gruesome avocation caused two great Bird Island tragedies in 1901 and 1910. Bird Island Keeper Bill Whalen and his assistant, Joe Pigeon had been hunting all day far out on the ice-cakes when a storm struck. Unable to make it back to the island, Whalen and his young son who had joined them for the excitement, froze to death. Pigeon, near death, but determined to survive, fought wave after wave, jumping from one ice cake to another and reached Bird Island Lighthouse. There, he broke the tragic news to Mrs. Whalen that she had lost both husband and son. Together they had to run the lighthouse for over a month before help could arrive through the fields of floating ice.

Nine years later there was a similar catastrophe. Bird Island Keeper Tele Turbid, with his son and assistant keeper, Damien Deveaux were far out on the ice floe searching for seals, when a high wind broke the ice into bergs which floated away from shore. The keeper and his assistant froze to death, but young Turbid was discovered lying unconscious on an iceberg floating by Cape Breton. He was rescued, but he later died of exposure and frostbite. His last words to the fishermen that found him were, *"Please save Annie Deveaux at the lighthouse."* An icebreaker was dispatched, and Annie, after a month alone in the lighthouse, was presented the sad news of the deaths. She was relieved of her lighthouse duties.

To add to the dilemma of Canada's Bird Island Light, another Pigeon, brother to the one who almost froze to death in 1900, was placed in charge of the lighthouse fog cannon, and with John Turbid, uncle of the keeper who froze to death in 1910, they had to keep the cannon firing out to sea throughout the fog filled day. Tired of carrying one charge of gunpowder at a time from the lighthouse to the cannon, which was a government rule, Pigeon and Turbid's assistant Paul Chenel, decided to lower an entire barrel of gunpowder over the cliffs to the men at the fog cannon. On the next shot, the cannon backfired, the priming cap landed in the barrel of gunpowder, and everyone was blown to kingdom-come, including Turbid's little boy who was looking on. Turbid the keeper, however, survived by being tossed into the ocean, but he was badly burned. It is from these great tragedies that tales of the ghosts haunting Bird Island-Light originated. The people of the Magdalens are explicit in describing a headless ghost that floats over the water, and over the ice in winter time from Bird Island, its arms waving frantically, as if in need of assistance. Also, the frozen forms of children have been seen from the lighthouse window, walking over the icebergs. Wearing white luminous shrouds, they too wave their arms as in need of help. Sometimes seen is the ghost of a woman in white wandering about the island near the base of the lighthouse, but whose spirit she might be, no one dares guess – possibly Keeper Whalen's wife or Annie Deveaux, both whom, it is said, were never right in the head again after their keeper husbands froze to death on the icepacks and they were left alone to tend the lighthouse.

"Stuff gets mysteriously moved out here, things like tools disappear into thin air. There is a presence here, like someone is watching you all the time. Even though lots of people come out here and laugh about Old Ernie, all the strange things that have happened here couldn't be our imagination," and so were the final words of the last keeper of Ledge Lighthouse in New London, Connecticut Harbor in 1987, just before the lighthouse was automated. The square, Georgian brick lighthouse, sitting on water in the harbor, opened for operation in 1909 and was taken over by the Coast Guard in 1939. The last entry in the log, 1987, reads: "A *rock of slow torture, Hell on Earth...It's Ernie's domain now."* Although no one is quite sure who Ernie is, or was, it has been established that he was a keeper of Ledge Light in 1936, and that he and his wife had operated the light for only a few months when she began a flirtation with the skipper of the Block Island ferryboat. The ferryboat was obliged to stop at the lighthouse periodically to provide supplies to the couple. One day, when Ernie had rowed the short distance to shore to buy sundry items, placing his wife in charge of the light, he returned to find his wife gone-forever. She had run off with the Block Island ferryman, leaving Ernie alone to trim his wick. Love-sick and despondent, Ernie leapt from the

third-story window of the lighthouse and drowned, but when the new keeper arrived to take Ernie's place at Ledge Light, Ernie was still there, cleaning windows, swabbing floors, rearranging desk drawers and lockers. The new keeper complained to authorities, but his stories about the anguished spirit of Ernie, still keeping the light, fell on deaf ears. Ernie's replacement was soon replaced, but as each new keeper came to Ledge Light, the ghost stories about the diligent and seemingly disturbed Keeper Ernie persisted. A Coast Guard keeper's wife in 1940, reported to the local press that she awoke one evening with an old bearded man standing over her. *"He opened his mouth as if about to say something, but in a moment, he dissolved."* The woman's children had also seen the vision, which they said was of *"a tall lanky man who smelled like fish."* Possibly that's why Ernie's wife left him – he smelled like fish.

"I have been taught in the school of loneliness," wrote the retiring keeper of Skerryvore Light in Scotland. *"I have known the distracted feeling of leaving a loving wife and romping children behind. I have known what a relief means on one of the wildest wave-swept rocks, in being oft times trailed through the surf, and washed off the landing stage, have in absolute darkness, during sunny hours for those on shore, been closed up for weeks hearing nothing but the incessant thunder of the Atlantic's mighty waves crash against and over our bottle-like edifice, and the screams of the sea-gulls, as if taunting us in our lonely plight."*

The loneliness of lighthouse keeping has at times, caused some of these men and women to develop serious psychological problems, or intensified problems they might have already had when they came into lighthouse service. Insane or distraught keepers, like Ernie of Ledge Light, became apt subjects for haunting apparitions. Ernie, in fact, must share his notoriety with another Long Island Sound specter named Julius, who supposedly haunts Stratford Shoal Lighthouse, situated on an underwater reef midway between Long Island and the Connecticut mainland. A 60-foot gray granite tower, built in 1878, was home to more than a few unstable characters who could not tolerate the lonely life. Most noted was Julius Koster, assistant keeper in 1905, who in May of that year, locked himself into the lantern room and stopped the rotation of the light. Keeper Morel, locked out of his own lighthouse in the middle of the Sound, was at a loss as to what to do. Julius not only threatened to snuff out the lantern but to kill himself behind the locked door. It seemed all but impossible to Morrel to stop him from either endeavor. He did, however, after hours of pleading, persuade Julius to open the door to the lantern room, but as Morrel saved the light, Julius once again attempted to take his own life by jumping into the swift moving waters. Morrel once again saved him. Julius was then tied down and Morrel called for help. It was two days before help arrived and Julius was removed permanently from the lighthouse. Although he did not succeed in his suicide endeavor at the lighthouse, he did apparently succeed shortly thereafter in New York City. His spirit returned to the Stratford Shoal Light to harass subsequent keepers and their assistants. Be it Koster or not, a poltergeist who the keepers called Julius, raised havoc within the castle-like structure for many years thereafter. Doors slammed shut in the middle of the night, chairs thrown against the walls, as if by someone in a rage, unseen hands tearing posters from the circular walls and flinging hot pans of water from the stove. Such activities nearly drove perfectly sane Coast Guardsmen nearly out of their senses. Being government servicemen, however, the activities of Julius were not repeated by them to the outside world, nor were they reported to superior officers. The men merely accustomed themselves as best as possible to the periodic rages of Julius. The Coast Guard keepers were removed in 1969 and the lighthouse doors and windows were sealed shut. Yet, Stratford Shoal remains a navigational aid, her light today being solar-powered, but inside the circular stone walls, fishermen and sailors passing by middle ground, report hearing loud noises, thumps, bumps, and grinding sounds from inside the structure. The lighthouse service pays little heed to these reports, knowing full well that it is just Julius making these noises, sealed up as once was his desire, in the lantern-room, and just having one of his tantrums.

"Out to sea, on a rock eight miles from the nearest point of land...I have been a prisoner," wrote 14 year old Annie Bell Hobbs, back in 1876. "The island I live on is made up of nothing but rocks, without one foot of ground for trees, shrubs or grass. The broad Atlantic lies before and all around us... The inhabitants of this island consist of eight persons... There are three men, the three keepers of the light, whose duties are to watch the light all night, to warn the sailors of danger. There are two families of us, and in my father's family are five members...I turn my eyes and thoughts toward the mainland and think how I should like to be there..." Annie Bell had her wish a few years later, when the Maine Lighthouse Board considered Boone Island too dangerous for women and children and turned it into a "stag lighthouse station." It is the tallest lighthouse, 137-feet above the sea, and considered the most isolated in New England, and one of the most dangerous. Not only does the conical granite tower sway In a storm, but the 400 square yards it sits on is sometimes completely covered by the sea, with heavy boulders thrown against the front door. The first wooden lighthouse built in 1799 on Boon Island, some nine miles off York and Kittery, was destroyed by a storm in 1804. Rebuilt, it was washed away in another storm in 1811. A stronger and taller stone tower replacement was swept off the island in an 1831 storm, and again in 1851. The keeper's home and outhouses are often being flooded or washed off the island, with the keeper and assistants running to the tower for safety. Inside the lighthouse, there are 168 steps to the lantern and as Annie Bell commented, "it was quite tiresome to go up into the light a number of times during the day." The present light was constructed in 1852, and two years later, a Kittery sea captain named

Bill Williams took command and remained at the light for 27 years. *"When rough weather came seas swept Boon Island clean,"* he once reported, *"and I was always thinking what I would do to save my life should the entire station be washed away. In the 1888 famous storm, my assistants and I had to take refuge at the top of the tower for three days. Even the Portland Gale of '98 was just a breeze compared to the '88 storm."* The 1932 storm sent seventy-foot waves crashing over the island and almost toppled the lighthouse, but the Blizzard of 1978, was what the Coast Guard called *"the boon year."* It was when the entire island was inundated with ice and snow and actually sank underwater. The keepers, hiding in the tower, had to be removed by helicopter. It was shortly thereafter that Boon Island Light was automated, and no humans but lighthouse inspectors are now allowed on the island.

The lighthouse ghost at Boon Island has been seen by many, and is described to be a sad faced young woman shrouded in white. She is usually seen, either on the surrounding rocks, or in days of yore, on the long spiral stairway inside the tower, usually a few hours before a storm. She has been spotted by keepers and assistants, including Coast Guardsmen, but also by fishermen who sail close to the island. Their sightings are usually at dusk. On calm days she has been heard moaning from somewhere in the bowels of the lighthouse, and on stormy days, her bone-chilling screech can be heard over the wind from inside the tower. Some believe that the ghost was on the island of rock before the first lighthouse was built. In life, she was supposedly the mistress of Captain John Deane, whose ship NOTTINGHAM GALLEY crashed into the island in December of 1710. It was here that the crew survived by eating the flesh of their shipmates before being rescued by York fishermen. There is, however, no evidence that there was a woman aboard the NOTTINGHAM GALLEY.

The female ghost could be the result of shipwrecks at the Boon Island Ledge, where tragedy struck many times before and after the erection of the first lighthouse. Consensus is, however, that the spirit that haunts the island is that of Katherine Bright, who was brought as a newlywed to Boon Island by her lighthouse keeper husband in the 1830s. At the lighthouse only four months, a surge tide from a winter storm swept the island. In attempting to secure the island's only boat, the keeper slipped on the rocks, fell into the sea and drowned. Katherine managed somehow to pull his body back onto the island and drag it to the lighthouse. Unable to lift him up the lighthouse stairs, she left his frozen body at the foot of the stairs, and dutifully performed her husband's chores for five days and nights. The lamp was lit each night until the storm and flood tides subsided, then, York fishermen noticed the light was out at dusk and they sailed to the island. There they found Mrs. Bright sitting on the stairs, cradling the frozen corpse of her husband. It was obvious to the fishermen that she hadn't eaten or slept for days and was almost frozen to death herself. She and the corpse were taken to the mainland, but even after days of care, it was concluded by all who attended her that Mrs. Bright had lost her mind. She died only a few weeks after being rescued, and subsequent keepers, such as John Thompson and Nathaniel Baker in the mid-nineteenth century, began telling stories to visitors to the island about the roaming spirit of Boon Island's Lady in White. Her wispy form is still seen periodically floating over the slippery rocks at the base of the lighthouse and her unearthly screeching is heard over the howling wind.

Keeper Charlie Knight of Hendrick's Head Light, Maine, was walking the long beach below the lighthouse one winter evening in 1945, *"when I passed a dignified looking woman walking the beach in the opposite direction. Puzzled as to why such a woman was walking in this lonely section of Southport on such a cold evening, when I reached the post office, I mentioned it to the Postmaster, and he too had seen the woman. Next morning when the tide went out, her drowned body, weighted down with a flatiron, was found at the beach."."* The woman was buried at a local cemetery and nobody ever learned who she was. Her ghost, however, has been seen many times walking by the lighthouse since then, and like the Boon Island spirit, she is described as being young and beautiful, glowing white. *"She paces the beach,"* said Charlie Knight, *"as if following the beacon of the light."* Her footprints have been seen in the sand as well, always leading into the water. Some believe that the apparition is not of the mysterious dignified lady who drowned in 1945, but is that of the mother of a shipwrecked baby that was recovered alive in the surf by the Hendrick's Head Light Keeper in 1871. The sinking vessel was caught on the ledge about a half mile off shore, but the keeper had no way to get to her. He watched the ship go under in the midst of a March gale and then rummaged through the wreckage that floated in on the waves at the beach. One strange item he pulled in was two feather mattresses bound together with manila rope. Untying the bundle, he found wedged inside, a wooden box, and from within the box came a strange whining sound. The keeper called to his wife, and opening the box, they found a crying baby girl inside, dry but frightened and cold. They rushed her to the hearth of the lighthouse, and there the child remained with the keeper and his wife for the rest of her natural life. Her real shipwrecked mother, however, filled with grief and longing, supposedly continues to haunt the crescent beach beneath the lighthouse, still searching for her daughter who she set adrift from a sinking ship so many years ago.

Maine's most noted lighthouse ghost, however, seems to have no known history to her at all – only that she is a protective spirit, forever warning mariners of impending danger, but in the process, frightening them half to death. Her home is Ram Island at the entrance to Boothbay Harbor, and she is described as *"a woman in white waving a lighted torch over her head."* One boat owner recently reported, that off Ram Island, *"seeing her I spun my wheel just in time to avoid being dashed on the rocks.*" Another fisherman reported that there was a *"flash of lightning,"* and there standing on the reef at Ram Island, waving her hands as warning was *"this lady all in white, as if full of electricity...if it weren't for her, I would have struck the ledge,"* he said. *"I was in danger of running into the rocks,"* said a Damaris Cove fisherman, *"when I saw a burning boat near shore, about to smash on the rocks and in the boat was this woman, waving me away. I quickly changed direction. The next day I saw no trace of the burning boat or the mysterious woman."* Prior to a lighthouse being built at Ram Island at Fisherman's Passage in 1883, hermits who lived on the island would hang lanterns from the rocks on stormy nights in the 1700s, and when one self appointed hermit keeper died another good Samaritans hermit took his place, on through the mid 1800s. The first official lighthouse keeper was Sam Cavenor, who served from 1883 to 1912. Sam had five daughters who grew up on Ram Island, so possibly it is one of them who feels obliged to continue carrying the torch for her father after death. The light was automated in 1965, but the lighthouse and outbuildings quickly fell into disrepair. Possibly one of Maine's museums or preservation societies will save the old lighthouse and also keep alive the mysterious female lifesaving spirit of the island.

Another lifesaving spirit can be found at one of the most dangerous areas in Long Island Sound, Penfield Reef, a mile long rock hazard located one mile from Fairfield, Connecticut. The history of the ghost here is well documented, beginning three days before Christmas in 1916. Keeper of the 24-year old lighthouse, Fred Jordan, had departed the tower in the dory that day to visit his family ashore for the holidays. He left Assistant Keeper Rudy Iten in charge. Only 150 yards from the light, as Rudy Iten tells us, *"Jordan's boat capsized, but he managed to cling to the overturned boat. He motioned me to lower the station's sailboat, but on account of the heavy seas, it was impossible to launch the boat alone at first, but a few minutes later the wind died down and I managed to lower the boat safely, and started off after the keeper. He now had drifted one and a half miles from the light. Because of strong headwinds I had to give up and return to the lighthouse. I sent distress signals to several ships but none answered. I lost track of the keeper at three PM, he is probably lost."*

He was lost, forever and Rudy Iten took over his job as head keeper. It was Iten again two weeks later that reported, *"I saw a ghostly figure gliding down the tower stairs, then disappearing from view."* Iten also reported, *"that evening I checked the station log and it was open to the entry of December 22nd, the night of Keeper Jordan's death.* Also that night, *"the light is behaving badly, for no apparent reason."* Maybe Keeper Jordan was trying to spook Keeper Iten for not saving him from drowning, but for decades after the drowning and long after Rudy Iten had left his post, the ghost of Keeper Jordan was seen in and outside the lighthouse. Two boys fishing near the lighthouse in

1942, capsized and were near drowning when a pale-faced man pulled them onto the Penfield rocks. When they had gained their strength, they walked up to the lighthouse, expecting to find the keeper who saved them, but he wasn't there, and only a photo viewed by the boys a few days later, made them realize that it was the dead Keeper Jordan who had saved them. Another more recent incident occurred in fog, when a family lost in the Sound sailed their yacht too close to the reef without realizing it, but were *"guided by a mysterious looking figure in a dory who vanished once the yacht reached safety."* Many keepers up until 1971 when the light was automated, told of the specter of Keeper Jordan being seen in the lantern room gallery, or floating above the reef itself next to the lighthouse, usually just before a storm. After any tragedy or shipwreck, *"the light behaved strangely for no apparent reason."* In the log it was blamed on *"atmospheric conditions,"* but everyone knew that what the keeper was saying was that, *"Keeper Jordan's ghost was raising havoc with the light again."* Today, the Pensfield Reef Light looks like a ghost tower, all boarded up and falling to pieces, but possibly the spirit of Keeper Jordan is still there, ready to save the lives of any mariners who might wander too close to the reef.

It has been debated in mariners' circles that neither Ledge Light, New London nor Pensfield Reef are the most haunted lighthouses in Long Island Sound. Execution Rocks Light, at the western end of the Sound near Sands Point, New York, is often given that distinction, and although listed as a historical place on the National Register, its haunting history is quite hazy. Keepers Tom Buckridge and George Clarke, there before the light was automated, have related stories of moanings in the dark and the rattling of chains in the tower. Such spectral noises might be expected, however, considering the many thieves and murderers who were hanged at Execution Rock, mostly out of New York City, before and after the lighthouse was erected in 1850. In 1935, the corpses of four men and a woman were uncovered beside the lighthouse. Who all these people were remains a mystery, yet their spirits have only caused occasional disturbances and disruptions.

Point Lookout Light, guiding traffic into the Potomac and in and around Chesapeake Bay, has been advertised as *"The Most Haunted Lighthouse in America,"* and was the first to be investigated using scientific methods and instruments. A team of psychic researchers spent days and nights at the lighthouse in 1987 in an effort to contact the spirits that had been seen and heard there for over a century. One being the ghost of a woman wearing a long blue dress and white blouse, who was often seen floating above the lighthouse stairs. She moans an sighs, and once was heard to say in a whisper, *"This is my home."* It is thought that she might be the spirit of Ann Davis, who was the lighthouse keeper there for many years, and was wife of the first lighthouse keeper. After spending some fifty years at Point Lookout Light, lighting the lantern and standing by it every night and snuffing it out each morning, she was found dead there one afternoon in the lantern room still on duty. The research team concluded that she haunts the lighthouse and *"grieves because the beacon no longer shines over the waters."* Park Rangers who have taken over the duty to secure and protect the old lighthouse from vandals, often see spirits walking through the lighthouse. One ranger swore he saw Joseph Haney's ghost *"peering in the back door of the lighthouse one evening just before a storm. When I went to the door, seeing the figure of a sailor standing there, it drifted backwards and disintegrated into the porch screen."* Joseph Haney was an officer aboard the steamer EXPRESS that wrecked offshore, and his body drifted onto the lighthouse rocks after the great storm of 1878. He now seemingly appears at the lighthouse door before every oncoming major storm. Another ranger who saw his apparition in December of 1977 said, *"I first heard his footsteps, then heard his clothes rustle, and looking up, I saw him standing there in uniform, blue* and *white, with brass buttons, eyes hollow and hair stringy wet, as if he just came out of the sea."* Graves have been found in and around the lighthouse at Point Lookout, some 4,000 of them. They are mostly Civil War soldiers' graves, for Point Lookout was a hospital and prison camp during the Civil War. It is filled with uneasy spirits, and especially now that the lighthouse stands in disrepair and abandoned, the ghosts are known to howl at night, and are heard by passengers and crews on passing vessels.

One lighthouse which can certainly challenge Point Lookout as the most haunted in the nation, is Block Island's Southeast Light off the Rhode Island coast. It is situated over 200-feet up on the edge of Monhegan Bluff and recently it almost toppled over the bluff into the sea. But, with herculean effort and 2.3 million dollars, the 200-ton brick tower was moved 245-feet back from the eroding edge in 1993. Unpredictably, the old lady ghost that has haunted the lighthouse for over one hundred years, moved with it. Like in so many lighthouse ghost stories, it seems that one of the first keepers of the light couldn't stand living alone with his wife at such a lonely station. Maybe she was a nag, or just talked too much, or possibly had a piano too, that drove her husband batty. At any rate, the keeper finally picked her up and threw her down the spiral stairs from the lantern room and killed her. He called it suicide, but he was convicted of murder. She, however, remained on duty in spirit form. She has harassed every keeper of the light in one form or another since her death, but she has not and apparently will not in any way, bother females who work at or visit the lighthouse. Nor does she molest children, although children have seen and heard her from time to time, banging pots and pans about the kitchen, or making an audible fuss. She is quite outspoken and physical, lifting beds with men in them and shaking them violently, locking men into rooms or closets, and once chasing a keeper out of his bed and into the cold night in his underwear. She then locked the lighthouse door behind him. Frightened and embarrassed, the near-nude keeper had to call the Coast Guard to reopen the lighthouse to let him in. The lighthouse move seems to have angered the old woman ghost, for she now rushes up and down the spiral stairs as if in a rage, and throws items about in seeming frustration. She also rearranges furniture, and has been known to throw bits of food at anyone who sits down to eat at the lighthouse kitchen. This is her domain and she is not bashful about letting the men know that she is in charge of Southeast Light. Her name, it is said, was Maggie Brown, but the Coast Guardsmen keepers call her *"Mad Maggie."*

To my way of thinking, the most haunted lighthouse on America's East Coast is my own lighthouse that sits some six miles out into the harbor from my backyard in Salem, Massachusetts. It is the Baker's Island Light, facing Halfway Rock and the open sea. Here it is not the lighthouse that is so possessed by ghosts, but the foghorn, which I can hear every misty or snowy evening, moaning over the wind in 15-second intervals. It was Andy Jerome and his wife Ruth, recent caretakers of the island, responsible for the lighthouse and fogbell as well, who first made me aware that the foghorn was haunted. *"It would go on for no reason on crystal clear nights,"* said Andy. *"I had to walk almost across the island from the caretaker's quarters to the lighthouse, where the horn was locked up, to shut it off. Every time I got right to the door of the outbuilding where it was blaring away, it would stop. This happened more than a dozen times each winter, and it would always stop just before I entered the little building behind the lighthouse where it is housed. I'm talking about cold nights, sometimes below zero, when there wasn't a cloud in the sky, nor a patch of fog around to set off the sensor. It was like the foghorn got lonely and wanted company, but all it needed was to see me at the door and it was comforted. The Coast Guard would inevitably send repairmen out to fix it, but they would find nothing wrong, and had no explanation as to why it sounded."*

History reveals that the old lighthouse keeper Walter Rogers, had similar problems with the Bakers Island fogbell, as Jerome did with the foghorn. Prior to a fogsiren being installed in 1906. a loud fogbell, operated by an automatic mechanism, was located on the rocks below the lighthouse. It once clanked loudly every half minute for 72 hours without a hitch, but it was hit by lightening on August 1, 1877, and never ran right again. It was replaced, but the new bell kept failing, which forced Keeper Rogers to leave his post in the lighthouse and spend hours in the damp fog banging the bell with a hammer. On July 16, 1879, the bell tower was once again demolished by a bolt of lightening and was replaced by a third bell. But this one was even more temperamental, being instrumental, some islanders say, in having Rogers leave his post as lighthouse keeper within two years.

Seventeen years later on July 4, 1898, Rogers returned to Bakers Island for a holiday picnic. With sixty others he left the island in late afternoon to return to Salem on the steamer SURF CITY. For some unknown reason the fogbell started ringing automatically as the steamer left the island. Leaving a few picnickers at Salem Willows, the steamer started for Beverly Harbor but was greeted by a great waterspout. It lifted the SURF CITY out of the water and tipped her upside down. She sank within a few minutes, drowning eight people, but the old keeper survived. Some believe the fogbell had tried to warn Keeper Rogers of the coming disaster. Ironically the bell of Bakers was struck by lightening again later that day and was destroyed.

"The lighthouse and the little foghorn building are haunted," says Ruth Jerome, Andy's wife. *"I'm very skeptical about this kind of thing, but every time I had to walk over to that part of the island, it raised the hackles on the back of my neck. It's like there is some kind of presence there. It wasn't that I was afraid to be over there, 'cause I wasn't, but it did give me a creepy feeling. I never felt frightened when I was alone out there but I never felt alone either, if you know what I mean."*

It may be, of course, that in one way or another, all lighthouses are haunted, some by quiet unobtrusive ghosts and others by lively spirits like the ones mentioned here. There's hardly a keeper alive today, no matter how sober and conservative a man or woman he or she night be, that wouldn't admit to feeling a chill now and then, or a feeling of another's presence in their midst during those late night vigils in the lantern room. Bernice Richmond, once keeper of Winter Harbor Light, two miles to sea in Frenchman's Bay, Maine, admits to often seeing things that weren't there and hearing voices of invisible people. Her brother Arthur, who had come to visit her in the lighthouse blamed his spooky feelings on the lighthouse cats. *"I was sitting here reading last night,"* he told his sister, *"and first one and then the other cat rushed to the window lashing its tail, listened and glared into the darkness as though it saw something outside, and I swear I heard voices downstairs after I went to bed. I don't understand how you stay here alone so much,"* he said. Bernice replied that, *"The cats undoubtedly saw something, and I hear voices often."* Bernice said she sometimes had *"unseen callers"* at the lighthouse. *"They seemed to be a mixed group of people who came down the walk under my window chatting casually, their feet audibly scraping the cement. They knocked at the back door in a moderate way and talked among themselves as they waited for me to come and open it. My callers weren't discouraged because I wouldn't open the door and repeated the knocks several times before going away. I don't know yet where my unreal callers came from or why they gave up knocking."* As Keeper Bernice Richmond knew from prior experience, if she went to the door, nobody would be there. Bakers Island caretaker Ruth Jerome said it all, when she said, *"I never felt frightened when I was alone out there, but I never felt alone out there either."*

Bibliography available by sending a stamped, self addressed envelope to the publisher.

Four of America's most haunted lighthouses: (top) Ledge Light, New London, Connecticut; (right) Bird Island Light, Marion, Massachusetts; (lower left) Southeast Light, Block Island, Rhode Island, and (lower right) Boon Island Ledge Light, Maine the tallest and possibly the most dangerous lighthouse in New England.
U.S. Coast Guard photos.